The Social Fashioning *of* Teacher Identities

Rethinking Childhood

Joe L. Kincheloe and Janice A. Jipson
General Editors

Vol. 25

PETER LANG
New York • Washington, D.C./Baltimore • Bern
Frankfurt am Main • Berlin • Brussels • Vienna • Oxford

Monica Miller Marsh

The Social Fashioning *of* Teacher Identities

PETER LANG
New York • Washington, D.C./Baltimore • Bern
Frankfurt am Main • Berlin • Brussels • Vienna • Oxford

Library of Congress Cataloging-in-Publication Data

Miller Marsh, Monica.
The social fashioning of teacher identities / Monica Miller Marsh.
p. cm. — (Rethinking childhood; vol. 25)
Includes bibliographical references and index.
1. Early childhood teachers—Attitudes. 2. Early childhood teachers—
Psychology. 3. Multicultural education. I. Title. II. Series.
LB1775.6 .M55   372.11—dc21   2001023435
ISBN 0-8204-5559-8
ISSN 1086-7155

Die Deutsche Bibliothek-CIP-Einheitsaufnahme

Miller Marsh, Monica:
The social fashioning of teacher identities / Monica Miller Marsh.
–New York; Washington, D.C./Baltimore; Bern;
Frankfurt am Main; Berlin; Brussels; Vienna; Oxford: Lang.
(Rethinking childhood; Vol. 25)
ISBN 0-8204-5559-8

*The author thanks Taylor & Francis Limited for their permission to reprint:
'The Shaping of Ms. Nicholi: The Discursive Fashioning of Teacher Identities'
by Monica Miller Marsh © 2002 International Journal of Qualitative Studies
in Education (forthcoming) http://www.tandf.co.uk*

Cover design by Dutton & Sherman Design

© 2003 Peter Lang Publishing, Inc., New York
275 Seventh Avenue, 28th Floor, New York, NY 10001
www.peterlangusa.com

All rights reserved.
Reprint or reproduction, even partially, in all forms such as microfilm,
xerography, microfiche, microcard, and offset strictly prohibited.

For my parents, Joyce Milarcik Miller and Gilbert Miller, who have always valued children and education. They have shown, by example, what can happen when adults provide children with possibilities.

And for my three wonderful nieces—Samantha, Alexandra, and Amelia—who continually bring joy to my life.

Contents

List of Tables		ix
Acknowledgments		xi
Chapter 1	The Social Nature of Teacher Thinking	1

Part I: The Discursive Fashioning of Ms. Nicholi

Chapter 2	Charting the Genre of Early Childhood Education	15
Chapter 3	An Early Childhood Teacher Education Program	28
Chapter 4	Woodlawn Elementary School	47
Chapter 5	Ms. Nicholi's Kindergarten	65

Part II: The Discursive Fashioning of Ms. Gonzales

Chapter 6	Charting the Genre of Multicultural Education	87
Chapter 7	A Multicultural Teacher Education Program	98
Chapter 8	Fernway Elementary School	112
Chapter 9	Ms. Gonzales' First Grade	130
Chapter 10	Implications for Early Childhood Educators	150

Notes	159
References	161
Index	167

List of Tables

3.1.	Professional Sequence of Courses Taken in the Early Education Program	30
3.2.	EEP Themes as Defined Within a Distinct Discourse	43
3.3.	EEP Teacher in Relation to Children, Families, and Colleagues	44
7.1.	Professional Sequence of Courses Taken in the Equity Academy	101
7.2	EA Program Themes as Defined Within a Multicultural Social Reconstructionist Discourse	108

Acknowledgments

I am reminded on a daily basis as I speak, act, and interact that identities are relational. My identities as researcher, teacher educator, and advocate for children have been shaped by each one of those who have shared their time, energy, and expertise with me. I would like especially to thank Beth Graue for her guidance and support throughout this project. She is an exemplary scholar, who continues to be a role model.

I owe special thanks to my editor, Janice Jipson, and to Mary Louise Gomez, Gloria Ladson Billings, Marianne Bloch, Mary Haywood Metz, Reba Page, Ken Teitelbaum, Lisa Loutzenheiser, Kathy Zozakiewicz, Margot Vagliardo, and Debbie Steers Van Hamel, whose insights and thoughtful questions have helped me to think more critically about my work.

Tamara Lindsey and Don Reynolds continuously read, critiqued, discussed, and motivated me to continue with my work through the long process of editing. Our relationship is the ultimate example of the social nature of thinking. Thank you!

Special thanks to Faye Story who provided the support at home so that I could find the time and space to write. Extra special thanks to Jeff Marsh, who has generously shared his love, encouragement, and sense of humor. He respected the time and effort that went into this book yet continually reminded me that the world was much larger than the one I was crafting on these pages.

I am grateful to all of the educators who took the time to participate in this study, especially Ms. Nicholi and Ms. Gonzales. They opened up their classrooms and their lives to me. Without their willingness to share their experiences and their struggles as first-year teachers, this book would not have been possible. I am also grateful for the Dr. Nuala McGann Drescher grant that provided the support to complete this book.

CHAPTER ONE

The Social Nature of Teacher Thinking

My first full-time teaching job was as a fifth grade teacher of gifted children in a northeastern Ohio school district with a long history of racial integration. Two years later, I moved into a full-day kindergarten position that became available in a neighboring district with a very similar history and student population. Both of the districts had experienced large demographic shifts during the 1980s. The elementary school in which I taught kindergarten had been comprised of a middle and upper-middle class, mainly white population ten years prior to my arrival. At the time I was hired to teach kindergarten the white population hovered slightly under 35 percent. Although the student body had changed dramatically, the teaching population remained fairly stable. The district was one of the highest-paying in the area, and most of my colleagues were near retirement.

In the three years that I taught kindergarten in this district, children, parents, and teachers became more and more frustrated with one another. I, too, was frustrated working with teachers who had good intentions but often did not acknowledge that the children they were teaching were much different from those children who they had taught in the past. My colleagues were supportive, caring, hard-working professionals who were just as frustrated about the issues that we were facing as I was. When I arrived, veteran teachers said such things to me as, "These kids don't want to work. I give a homework assignment, and half of them won't complete it." These kids don't have any support from their parents. The parents don't value education, so why should they?" "They want us to change our teaching strategies for these kids. Why should I change my teaching? It worked for fifteen years."

Although I certainly did not have answers for the problems that my district was facing, I knew that there were ways of instructing and creating curriculum that would address this new population. I had been reading the multicultural literature that was gaining in prominence at this time and made the decision to enter a doctoral program so that I could explore the methods for instruction and curriculum development for teaching diverse groups of children. I began thinking about focusing my efforts in the area of teacher education. I believed that prospective teachers, unlike the teachers with whom I was working, would enter teaching with minds that were open to a multicultural approach.

Throughout my doctoral work, I was fortunate enough to teach courses to prospective teachers who were working toward certification in early childhood education. One of the courses that I was teaching was a social studies methods course that included a field component. I was particularly enthusiastic about the opportunity to work with students who were actually interacting with children in elementary schools. However, by the third week of the course, my enthusiasm had begun to wane. One of the requirements of the course was that students keep a reflective journal of their classroom experiences. I was disheartened to read comments like the following:

> *The child that I do not connect with is African American. She comes from a broken home and is economically disadvantaged. She has a lot of problems in school because of her social skills. I believe that she has experienced a lot of bad things in her life. She acts very hostile and aggressive. I think the biggest factor in our relationship has to do with how she's been raised.*

> *There is one child, a girl, in my classroom who I really do not connect with at all. She is just very hard for me to relate to because I can never tell what she is thinking. She is just not with the program. . . . I think that she comes from a bad family situation. I wish I could get through to her and make her see the value of following classroom rules and working together, she seems so egocentric.*

I had not expected the journal entries written by prospective teachers to reflect the same sentiments that had been articulated by the practicing teachers with whom I had taught. That week in class, after asking for permission, I read some of these journal entries aloud. I then asked how many of my students had had an opportunity to meet the parents of the children. Not one student had interacted or spoken with the parents that they had written about in their journals. While some said that their cooperating teachers had shared this information about student families, other articulated that they were just hypothesizing that this was why the students were acting this way. Looking at the group of 26 white female teachers sitting before me was, in many ways, like looking into a mirror. I began to question the origins of my own thoughts about teaching. I knew that some of the techniques of teaching, such as the various ways of presenting instruction to children, how to create a lesson that attracted and maintained the attention of young children, and how to plan and implement curriculum had come from my teacher education program. But what about my perceptions of children and their families? Further, why did I make the decisions about curriculum and instruction that I did?

So began my quest to understand why and how teachers come to think about children, teaching, and learning in the ways that they do. I began to search the literature on the topic of teacher thinking and found that educational researchers have been trying to capture its essence for over two decades. Studies have ranged in focus from scrutinizing the cognitive processes of teachers' instructional planning to collecting and examining personal histories. Although some scholars in the field of education have conceptualized the relationship between teacher thought and action as linear and unidimensional (Clark & Peterson, 1986), others argue that teacher thinking is a dialectical process (Clandinin & Connelly, 1987) composed of multiple factors that often work in opposition to one another. Despite differences in assumptions about the nature and characteristics of teacher thinking, the primary object of investigation has traditionally been the individual teacher. Recently, a small number of educational scholars have shifted the focus of teaching away from the individual teacher and have begun to explore the social nature of teacher thinking (Britzman, 1991; Casey, 1993; Danielewicz, 2001; Gomez, in press; Miller Marsh, 2002). It is the notion of teacher thinking as a collective venture rather than an individual enterprise and its implications for teacher education that this book explores.

Teacher Thinking as Unidimensional

Early studies of teacher thinking focused primarily on the thought processes that teachers employed during instructional planning (Carter, 1990; Clark & Peterson, 1986; Shavelson & Stern, 1981). Researchers investigating the types, functions, and planning routines that were established by individual teachers worked to construct models of cognition. A number of educational scholars conducted research which supported the notion that instructional planning guided practical action (Carnahan, 1980; Peterson, Marx & Clark, 1978; Zahorik, 1970). These scholars believed that if educational researchers could discover and depict the psychological frameworks of effective teachers then generalizations could be made to the entire teaching population. The goal of this research was to "determine the points and parameters of teachers' choices about their actions" (Carter, 1990, p. 297).

A positivistic approach to research was prevalent in the social sciences at this time, and research conducted in the field of teacher education was no exception. Instructional planning research was conducted in laboratory-like settings. Data were collected through the use of such methodologies as policy capturing, stimulated recall, simulations, and checklists. Educational scholars rarely involved teachers in discussions or analyses concerning their own practice.

As information was compiled on the topic of instructional planning, some educational researchers recognized that teaching was a much more complex process than merely organizing and implementing educational instruction. Research findings illustrated that although teachers developed elaborate plans, they readily altered their instruction based on events that occurred inside their classrooms (Morine-Dershimer, 1979; McCutcheon, 1980). These findings refuted earlier claims that teacher thinking was a linear process. Rather, this group of researchers, rejecting the dichotomy between thought and action that had dominated earlier work, conceptualized teacher thinking as dialectical. They argued that opposing and contradictory forces, such as the interactions that took place between students and teachers, informed and shaped teacher thought and action. Educational studies were based on the notion that teacher thinking was dialectically focused on patterns of interaction, teacher judgments, and decision making.

Teacher Thinking as Dialectical

The notion that teacher thinking was a dialectical process generated a variety of new questions. The generation of these questions was made possible in part by the shifting nature of educational research. Positivistic approaches to the social sciences were being replaced by interpretive perspectives. Interpretive researchers relied on methodological tools that allowed them to conduct their research in actual classroom environments rather than in artificially created settings. Case studies, ethnographies, and interviews with teachers became much more prominent. As researchers began spending more time with teachers in school contexts, they became aware of a more personal dimension of teacher thinking.

The personal dimension of teacher thinking comprises emotional, moral and aesthetic components. A small but growing number of scholars turned their attention to the study of teachers' implicit theories and personal knowledge (Connelly & Clandinin, 1985; Elbaz, 1983; Munby, 1982). From this perspective, individual teacher thinking was conceptualized as a composition of "ongoing action and personal experience" (Clandinin & Connelly, 1987, p. 494).

In an effort to understand the influence of the personal on an individual teacher's practice, researchers began working much more closely with teachers. They encouraged individual teachers to bring forth their tacit knowledge and the theories that guided their practice through the articulation of their personal histories. Personal data were collected in a variety of forms, including a wide array of narrative methods, such as life stories, life histories, biographies, and autobiographies. These were often collected in tandem with classroom data in order to make connections between past experience and present practice. In some instances, researcher and teacher worked together to create a language of praxis that superseded the artificial separation between the theoretical discourse of the academy and the discourse of classroom practice (Connelly & Clandinin, 1985). Researchers such as Connelly and Clandinin argued that it is impossible to separate the thoughts of an individual from his/her personhood. Rather than building models of what teachers know, researchers attempted to explain how teachers learn as they teach and how that knowledge is enacted in a variety of teaching situations.

An awareness of the constraints and the possibilities that a given school context defined for an individual teacher emerged from the work on personal practical knowledge. Although the instructional planning, decision making, and interactions of individual teachers do occur in very distinct and personal ways, the composition of a classroom, school, or community dictates to a significant degree what a teacher can and cannot do within the confines of her classroom. The emergence of a body of literature pertaining to classroom knowledge contends that teacher thinking is "situated" and "grounded in the common experience of classroom events" (Carter, 1990, p. 302). Educational researchers in this area examine how individual teachers negotiate their social contexts and explore the relationships among the ever-changing events that take place in a classroom environment and the knowledge, organization, and comprehension of an individual teacher (Carter, 1990). Researchers look for patterns and common themes across teaching situations in order to understand how heavily contextual factors shape teacher thought and action.

A Different Perspective on Teacher Thinking

In this study I move away from the traditional teacher thinking research with its focus on the individual teacher and move toward a view of teaching that conceives of teacher thought as a collective enterprise. A growing body of literature has shown that schools and families are shaped by the cultural forces that are present in a given community (Graue, 1993; Heath, 1983; Hemmings & Metz, 1990; Lareau, 1989; Metz, 1989). These cultural forces include the increasing pressures of school reform, the values of the community in which a school is located, the relationships among teachers in a given school context, and the individual belief systems and values of a given teacher (Graue & Miller Marsh, 1996). The juxtaposition of this research with that on teacher thinking problematizes the notion that teacher thinking is an individual enterprise. Rather, it suggests that teacher thinking is heavily influenced by societal and local beliefs about schooling.

Instead of linear or dialectic, teacher thought should be considered dialogic (Bakhtin, 1986). Teacher thinking is an ongoing dialogue among one's personal history, present conditions, beliefs, values, and the social, cultural, historical, and political forces that surround groups of individuals in a given time and place. The threads that comprise this dialogic web of relations are constantly shifting as they come into contact with one another. Unlike the notion of dialectics, in which oppositional forces come into play between people, a dialogic relationship occurs on interindividual territory (Volosinov, 1973), the space where self and other converge.

From this perspective, teacher thinking is a melange of past, present, and future meanings that are continually being negotiated and renegotiated through social interaction.

A Theoretical Framework for Studying Collective Teacher Thought

If teacher thinking is conceived as being dialogic in nature, it would seem worthwhile to attempt to develop an understanding of how ideologies of teaching are shaped by the forces present in a specific community and how they become inscribed in the thoughts and actions of individual teachers. The work of two Russian theorists and colleagues, Valentin Volosinov and Mikhail Bakhtin, are helpful in this regard.

The theoretical writings of Volosinov and of Bakhtin emphasize the socially constructed nature of existence. The work produced by both theorists highlights the role that language plays in shaping the relations between and among people. Language in this context is conceptualized as being much more than simply a system of grammatical rules and structures. For Bakhtin and Volosinov, language is a living, dynamic force that allows human beings to interact with one another while simultaneously creating their world. Rather than focus on the structural aspects of language, Bakhtin and Volosinov explore the conceptual and political dimensions that provide frameworks for thought and action.

The work of Volosinov (1973) on the concept of ideologies with that of Bakhtin (1986, 1981) on speech genres creates a theoretical framework that explains how ideologies are social constructions that both shape and are shaped by individual and collective thought. Volosinov's theory highlights the need to explore how language is a carrier of ideology, but it is Bakhtin who provides the unit of language to study. Bakhtin contends that participation in meaningful conversation depends on an individual's ability to recognize and interact with others in highly specific spheres of communication. Bakhtin terms these spheres of shared language *speech genres*. Speech genres are forms of language that allow like-minded speakers to understand one another and provide them with the common ground on which to create and exchange ideas.

Theoretical Contributions of Bakhtin and Volosinov

Individuals communicate with one another in a common language. The words that they use and the meanings attached to them are created socially as the history of their relations evolve over time. Individuals access a speech genre each time they think, speak, write, or interact with others. Bakhtin (1986) contends:

> In the genre the word acquires a particular typical expression. Genres correspond to typical situations of speech communication, typical themes, and, consequently, also to particular contacts between the meanings of words and actual concrete reality under typical circumstances. (p. 87)

The number of speech genres is infinite. Genres range from those that are attached to specific families to those that circumscribe specific institutions such as churches, schools, or governments. Without genres to guide speech and action, individuals in groups would be unable to communicate in meaningful ways with one another.

Genres are comprised of a multiplicity of discourses that weave in and through one another as they travel through time and space. Discourses, like genres, are frameworks for thought and action that groups of individuals draw upon in order to speak and interact with one another in meaningful ways. Discourses, like genres, are historically, culturally, politically, and socially generated patterns of thinking, speaking, acting, and interacting that are sanctioned by a particular group of people (Fairclough, 1989; Burman, 1994; Gee, 1996). But genres are much broader than discourses. Multiple discourses become tangled together to make up the spheres of communication that Bakhtin refers to as speech genres.

Discourses are continually in motion. They become knotted together and then unraveled as they bring together fragments of ideologies that generate new meanings yet never allow old intentions to fade away completely. As discourses knit together and become unified they become speech genres. However, just as genres are continually in the process of being unified, they are also continually in the process of being stratified.

Stratification occurs as social, cultural, political, and historical forces work together to pull language apart as it struggles to become unified and whole. The forces continually being exerted on language to unify and stratify produce the dynamic that keeps language alive and ever-changing. The process of stratification further splinters genres into layers of language such as those that are tied to professions, social groups, or particular generations. At any given time, in any social sphere, language is a site of contention. The divergent points of view inherent in past, present, and future meanings clash as they struggle for ideological (and material) predominance.

In order to attain membership in a given group, an individual must appropriate one or more of the discourses that flows in and through the community and become proficient at negotiating meaning and actions within the genres' borders. As individuals become immersed in social communities, they appropriate the ways of thinking, speaking, and interacting that provide them access to group membership. This may involve a great deal of internal struggle because individuals are already replete with meanings and intentions that reflect particular beliefs, values, and ways of viewing the world. Volosinov explains that this struggle is negotiated on "interindividual territory" (Volosinov, 1973).

The creation of a self's consciousness takes place on interindividual territory and therefor is both a social and an individual act. Ideologies are diffused among individuals as they encounter one another socially. Volosinov (1973) asserts:

> This ideological chain stretches from individual consciousness to individual consciousness, connecting them together. Signs emerge, after all, only in the process of interaction between one individual consciousness and another. And the individual consciousness itself is filled with signs. Consciousness becomes consciousness only once it has been filled with ideological (semiotic) content, consequently, only in the process of social interaction. (p. 11)

As ideologies enter into an individual's consciousness, they encounter an ideological system that is already in place. This internal ideology or individual consciousness is created in the context of an individual's life. It is the "whole aggregate of conditions of life and society in which that organism has been set" (Volosinov, 1973, p. 35). According to Volosinov (1973) the individual consciousness is the space where biology, biography, and ideology intersect. It is here that individuals process their understanding of experiences and put their "individual imprint" on their thoughts, actions, and ways of being in the world (Volosinov, 1973).

This process of socially negotiating various ideological representations of the self is the act of constructing identities. Identities are created through dialogue on interindividual territory. Discourses interact with one another to shape how individuals perceive the world and to position them within it. Just as language is fluid and perpetually shifting so are identities. As Kondo (1990) explains:

> Rather than universal essences, selves are rhetorical assertions, produced by our linguistic conventions, which we narrate and perform for each other. Identities on the individual level resist closure and reveal complicated, shifting, multiple facets. And selves [are] never separable from context. (p. 307)

In other words, we are continually in the process of fashioning and refashioning our identities by patching together fragments of the discourses to which we are exposed. Yet, we do not have complete choice over how we craft our selves. Bakhtin tells us that some discourses beckon to us to immerse ourselves in them while other discourses impose themselves upon us. He refers to these two distinct types of discourses as *internally persuasive* and *authoritative,* respectively.

Bakhtin explains that the discourses imposed upon us are those that are tethered to scientific, religious, or political power and are imbued with authority. Bakhtin (1981) describes these powerful discourses as *authoritative*.[1] He writes (p. 342), "The authoritative word demands that we acknowledge it, that we make it our own; it binds us, quite independently of any power it might have to persuade us internally; we encounter it with its authority already fused to it." Authoritative discourses are not negotiable. They are surrounded by borders that are stable and fixed. According to Bakhtin the authority embedded within these discourses is so great that we must either totally affirm or totally reject them.

Bakhtin refers to those discourses in which individuals choose to engage as *internally persuasive* (Bakhtin, 1981). Internally persuasive discourses are mutable and ever-changing. As they become entangled with each other, they create spaces for creativity and liberation (Bakhtin, 1981, p. 348). These are the spaces in which new configurations of ideas, beliefs, and values are imagined.

The crafting of identities, when drawing on discourses, whether they are internally persuasive or authoritative, is always relational. Conceptualizing the construction of the self as relational means that choosing to author one's self-identities in particular ways simultaneously creates possibilities and constraints for the identities of those with whom one is in relationship. Thus, understanding how teachers fashion their identities is especially important, since much of the work that is done in classrooms by teachers and their students involves the crafting of identities with and for one another.

Definitions of the Terminology

The interrelated terms ideology, discourse, speech genre, and identities will be used throughout this text. It is important to understand the specific links among these concepts and the ways they work together to shape both the verbal and material lives of individuals.

Ideologies are "representations of reality" that are embedded in discourses. Rather than simply being systems of ideas or beliefs, ideologies are historically produced practices in which power and authority are implicit (Shapiro, 1988). Ideologies become inscribed in an individual's consciousness to structure how that individual views the world and is positioned within it. Because ideologies are lived out in the practices of everyday life they appear to be natural and permanent (Shapiro, 1988). These naturalized views of the world mask the socially constructed nature of "reality" and allow the existing social order to be unquestioningly reproduced (Shapiro, 1988).

A discourse is a pattern of thinking, speaking, behaving, and interacting that is socially, culturally, and historically constructed and sanctioned by a specific group or groups of people. The particular beliefs, values, and world views held by a given group are embedded in discourses. In other words, discourses are suffused with ideologies. Discourses operate in and through individuals to structure experiences, interactions, social relations, daily practices, and ways of being in the world.

Speech genres are spheres of communication that like-minded individuals draw upon in order to communicate in meaningful ways with one another. They are comprised of a multiplicity of discourses that become woven together, then pull apart as they travel through time and space.

Identities can be thought of as ideological representations of the self. They are negotiated through social interaction and therefore are perpetually in a state of flux.

A Study of the Social Nature of Teacher Thinking

This book explores how teacher thinking and, ultimately, how teacher identities are shaped through social interaction in the various contexts through which first-year teachers move. It is based on a study of how two first-year teachers were shaped through their interactions with peers and faculty in their university courses, parents, children, teachers, and other staff members in elementary school settings, remnants of ideologies from their past schooling experiences, and the broader social, cultural, historical, and political forces of their lives. By juxtaposing the social aspect of ideology with the personal aspects of a teacher's life, it is possible to locate the interface between self and other where the crafting of identities takes place.

To explore the ways in which teacher thought is socially constructed yet individually enacted, I gathered data on both a social and an individual level. On a social level, I attempted to identify the discourses that enveloped the teacher education programs, the elementary school contexts and the classroom in which each teacher was situated. By developing an understanding of the discourses that flowed through each context, it was possible to identify the specific ideologies of teaching that the first-year teachers appropriated as they fashioned their teacher identities. At the individual level, I employed ethnographic and narrative techniques to make sense of how the biographies of these teachers shape and are shaped by their ideologies of teaching.

The Structure of the Book

The book is divided into two distinct sections. Part I discusses the discursive fashioning of Ms. Anne Nicholi, a first-year kindergarten teacher. Part II centers on the discursive fashioning of a first year, first-grade teacher, Ms. Juniper Gonzales. These two focal teachers, as well as all faculty, students, schools, and communities discussed in this book, are given pseudonyms.

Part I consists of Chapters 2 through 5. Chapter 2 reaches back in time to briefly trace the development of some of the discourses that shape the genre of early childhood education. It explores how the social, cultural, and political forces in a given era have positioned groups of individuals, most specifically teachers, in particular ways. The focus of Chapter 3 is the Early Education Program, the undergraduate early childhood program from which Ms. Nicholi had been graduated. Woodlawn Elementary School, the school in which Ms. Nicholi works, is the focus of Chapter 4. Chapter 5 examines the interactions that take place among Ms. Nicholi and the children in her kindergarten and explores how her identities have been constructed by the language that she has appropriated from the EEP, Woodlawn elementary, and her personal life.

Part II is parallel in structure to Part I. Chapter 6, explores the evolution of multicultural education over time by tracing some of the prominent discourses that have shaped the genre. Chapter 7 identifies the discourse that comprises the genre of the Equity Academy, the graduate teacher education program that Ms. Gonzales attended. Chapter 8 discusses the competing discourses that comprise the context of Fernway Elementary school. Chapter 9 examines the context of Ms. Gonzales' first-grade classroom and the ways in which her identities have been discursively constructed by the multiple contexts through which she has moved.

Chapter 10 discusses the implications for teacher education of conceptualizing the nature of teacher thinking as a social endeavor rather than an individual enterprise.

given era have positioned groups of individuals, most specifically teachers, in particular ways. The focus of Chapter 5 is the Early Education Program, the undergraduate early childhood program from which Ms. Nicholl had been graduated. Woodbine Elementary School, the school in which Ms. Nicholl works, is the focus of Chapter 6. Chapter 7 examines the interactions that take place among Ms. Nicholl and the [illegible] her knowledge [illegible] and explores how her identities have been constructed by the language that she has appropriated from the [illegible]

[illegible] it is [illegible] Chapter [illegible] teacher education [illegible] the [illegible] Chapter [illegible] the discourses [illegible] the [illegible] education program that Ms. [illegible] Woodbine Elementary School. Chapter 9 [illegible] in which her identities have been [illegible] constructed by the [illegible] in which she has moved.

Chapter 10 discusses the implications for teacher education of conceptualizing the nature of teacher thinking as a social endeavor rather than an individual enterprise.

PART I

The Discursive Fashioning of Ms. Nicholi

CHAPTER TWO

Charting the Genre of Early Childhood Education

There is debate over the definition of early childhood education. Although many educational programs describe early childhood as the period of development spanning from kindergarten or preschool through third grade (Bredekamp, 1990), the National Association for the Education of Young Children (NAEYC), the largest professional early childhood organization, defines early childhood as the period from birth through age eight. This is based on both developmental and political principles (Bredekamp 1990). Developmentally, children from birth to age eight are believed to progress through a recognizable sequence of stages of growth and development. Politically, defining early childhood education through the third grade provides the field with a link to the benefits received by elementary school educators and also provides the early childhood community with a certain level of influence on the curriculum and instruction presented to children in the primary grades. For the purposes of this text, early childhood education refers to the age range of birth through eight. Specific ages will be highlighted as practices and policies shift over time.

Beginning with the colonial era, this chapter traces the development of the genre of early childhood education up through the present. It attempts to reach back in time and space to capture the discourses that shape the identities of the early childhood teacher in relation to the students and families with whom she works. The chapter illustrates how the authoritative discourses of religion and science are woven in and through the genre of early childhood education and become entangled with discourses of race, class, and gender to position children and teachers in particular ways. Each section begins with an epigraph so that the reader has a sense of not only the language and terminology in use at the time but also the tone of the discourse of that particular era.

Discourses of Morality and Religion

> ... poor as well as rich may be instructed in good and commendable learning, which is to be preferred before wealth. Be it enacted etc., That all persons in this Province and territories thereof, having children, and all the guardians and trustees of orphans, shall cause such to be instructed in reading and writing, so that they may be able to read the Scriptures and to write by the time they attain to twelve years of age. (General Assembly of Philadelphia 1683 in Wickersham, 1969, p. 39)

Out-of-home child care has been available to children in the United States in a variety of forms since the latter part of the seventeenth century (Bloch, 1987). The earliest schools were established for the purpose of teaching young children to read the Bible. During the colonial era, children were constructed as inherently evil beings in need of salvation (Bloch, 1987; Lightfoot, 1978; Weber, 1984). Parents were deemed responsible for teaching children moral and religious values as well as how to read and write. Discourses of social class constructed children from poor, immigrant, and less well-educated working-class families as morally lacking in relation to children from prosperous families. Wealthy children were educated at home by their parents or servants. These families also provided care and education for orphans and children who, they believed, were not receiving proper moral training. Schools were established for children as young as three in order to "rectify deficiencies of the home" (Bloch, 1987, p. 30).

Although discourses of class positioned the poor as morally deficient, discourses of race constructed those who were "nonwhite"[1] as biologically inferior (Frankenberg, 1994). In some instances, Negroes[2] who were forced into slavery were not even considered human beings (Cunningham & Osborn, 1979). The few schools that existed at this time for Indian and Negro children were founded by religious organizations. Conversion to Christianity was the impetus for the formation of these schools (Lightfoot, 1978).

Discourses of gender positioned females in the home at the center of domestic activity. Girls were rarely educated beyond basic reading and writing skills, and fewer girls than boys attended the early district schools (Lightfoot, 1978). Teachers in the early schools were most often males. For the majority of these men, teaching was a part-time job assumed to earn extra money. In rural areas, farmers taught during the winter months, and women were recruited to teach during the summer. In urban areas, men taught during breaks from the university or seminary (Hoffman, 1981). Older, usually widowed, women established another form of schooling for young children. These schools were referred to as dame schools. The female instructor would teach reading and writing to a small group of children for a nominal fee. Her home would serve as the base for this instruction (Bloch, 1987; Hoffman, 1981; Lightfoot, 1978).

Many teachers taught for only one term, and their qualifications were often questionable (Hoffman, 1981). This was not viewed as problematic, however, since the majority of the teacher's time was spent listening to textbook recitations, drilling students in spelling and arithmetic, and enforcing harsh discipline. This type of instruction would hardly require the teacher to form any positive or lasting relationships with students, for she was mired in discourses that positioned her as a moral conformist working towards rescuing her students and their families from the consequences of sin.

During the first half of the 1800s, the intertwined forces of industrialization, immigration, and urbanization in the North led to the growth of schooling in urban areas. Discourses that once shaped the child as inherently evil had become entwined with discourses of romanticism. The child was now constructed as innocent, pure, and naturally good (Weber, 1984). It was believed that all children needed to attend school. Schooling would save the white, middle-class child from "the race for wealth, luxury, ambition and pride," and the immigrant child from "the inherited stupidity of centuries of ignorant ancestors" (Hoffman, 1981, p. 12).

Educational leaders such as Johann Pestalozzi and Friedrich Froebel looked to the notions of the philosopher Jean Jacques Rousseau to guide their thinking. Childhood, for the first time, was defined as a distinctive stage in one's life (Cleverley & Phillips, 1986). Rousseau believed that in order to develop the power of reason for adulthood, children needed to be given the freedom to follow their natural and instinctive impulses (Cleverley & Phillips, 1986). Contradictorily, he advised parents and caregivers to manipulate learning environments so that children were provided with particular experiences yet were coerced into believing that they were choosing what they wanted to do.

Three new types of early childhood care emerged during this period: the infant school, the kindergarten, and the day nursery. Philanthropic and charity organizations comprised of white middle-class women sponsored all three types of early childhood programs and hired white, middle-class women[3] to teach. In spite of the shift in discourses that had redefined children as innocent and pure, discourses of social class continued to position poor and immigrant children as morally lacking in relation to their middle-class peers.

The infant school transplanted to the United States from England in the early 1800s became another vehicle for inculcating middle-class beliefs and values in poor and immigrant children. Infant schools provided an alternative to the harsh discipline and drill that was inflicted upon the young children who attended "common" schools, as the public schools were known at the time. Children between the ages of eighteen months and seven years were instructed in religion and morality as well as "sensory-oriented object lessons and play" (Bloch, 1987, p. 31). The infant school movement became so popular that middle-class mothers, fearful that their children would academically fall behind their lower-class peers, argued for the establishment of infant schools for their own children. The following excerpt published in the February 1828 edition of the *Ladies' Magazine* portrays the sentiments of the more prosperous at this time:

> The interesting subject of infant schools is becoming more and more fashionable. . . . We have been told that it is now in contemplation to open a school for the infants of others besides the poor. If such a course be not soon adopted, at the age for entering primary schools those poor children will assuredly be the richest scholars. And why should a plan which promises so many advantages, independent of merely relieving the mother from her charge be confined to children of the indigent? (in Bloch, 1987, p. 32)

By the 1840s large numbers of affluent children were enrolled in the infant schools and the curriculum shifted away from the playful, informally structured environment and moved towards academics and scholarship (Bloch, 1987). Controversy arose over issues of instructing such young children in reading and writing as well as over who should provide their care. Magazines and newspapers published articles suggesting that schooling for young children was dangerous for their health and that the best place for children to receive care was in the home with their mothers (Bloch, 1987). Public pressure forced white middle-class mothers to take their children out of infant schools and educate them at home. By 1870, the infant schools had declined in great numbers.

The attention of the philanthropists was drawn away from the infant schools and towards the newly emerging kindergartens. The kindergarten, conceptualized in Germany by Friedrich Froebel, was introduced to Watertown, Wisconsin, in 1865 by one of his students, Margarethe Schurz (Quam, 1988). Froebel proclaimed that the kindergarten was "the free republic of childhood" and that young children should be instructed by a warm, nurturing female in a home-like environment. He created a system of learning based on "natural" stages of development. Froebel believed that the newborn child held the potential for the "totally integrated and mature adult human being" (Watertown Historical Society, 1988). The child was to be nurtured through religious preparation and guided play. Froebel developed ten "gifts" to correspond to what he believed to be the "natural" stages of development. These consisted of a variety of shapes and forms that were found in nature such as cubes, cylinders, and balls. Gifts were presented to children in order from simple to most complex. The sequence of introducing the gifts guided children from concrete to abstract thinking.

While the earliest kindergartens catered exclusively to children of the affluent, kindergartens also became the new training grounds for poor and immigrant children. Small numbers of colored children attended kindergartens alongside their white and immigrant peers, but strict quotas limited their enrollment (Cunningham & Osborn, 1979). It should be noted that kindergartens for colored children were established privately. Assimilation and the production of moral citizens were the goals of the kindergarten (Rothman, 1978). As one advocate stated, "The kindergarten is the great educational agent of this age, and is the only factor which will accomplish what all reformatory measures of the States have failed to do.... It is cheaper to support kindergarten than prisons" (New York State Charities Aid Association, 1888, in Rothman, 1978, p. 103).

Charity organizations were also responsible for founding day nurseries. Day nurseries were made available to working-class mothers of young children. For around five cents a day, working-class children were cared for, fed nutritious meals, and guided in religious and moral training (Rothman, 1978). Appropriating the gendered discourse that mothers belonged at home with their children, day nurseries would agree to keep children only on the days that the mother worked.

Contradictory discourses of gender placed middle-class mothers in their homes caring for their children as they simultaneously positioned single middle-class women in the nurturing and caring roles of teacher. Catherine Beecher was one of the leading figures who advocated for teaching as a profession for women. In *An Essay on the Education of Female Teachers,* Beecher wrote:

> It is woman, fitted by disposition, and habits, and circumstances for such duties, who, to a very wide extent, must aid in educating the childhood and youth of this nation; and therefore it is, that females must be trained and educated for this employment ... the education necessary to fit a woman to be a teacher, is exactly the one that best fits her for that domestic relation she is primarily designed to fill. (Beecher, 1835, in Rothman, 1978, p. 57)

According to Beecher and those who rallied around her argument, teaching school was training for future motherhood. They contended that women should fill the vacant positions men had left when they entered higher-paying, more prestigious jobs in industry (Apple, 1985; Hoffman, 1981). Male administrators and school board members embraced Beecher's argument. The idea of a cadre of compliant women who would transmit "American" ideals and values to poor and immigrant children for lower salaries than their male predecessors was very appealing (Grumet, 1988; Hoffman, 1981; Rothman, 1978).

Females who desired to teach were encouraged to become certified through teacher training programs. Programs for certification required a relatively long-term commitment that made teaching less attractive to their male counterparts (Apple, 1985; Hoffman, 1981). Training for kindergartners[4] initially took place in the kindergarten classroom. Prospective kindergartners were paired with practicing kindergartners and learned on site how to teach and care for young children (Spodek, 1988). As their positions became professionalized, they, like their common school colleagues, began to receive their training in normal schools.

Discourses of gender expanded opportunities for female teachers. Teaching provided young, single middle-class women with a new sense of independence.

Young women who chose to become teachers were able to live away from home, financially support themselves (many of them also contributed to the family income), and access higher levels of education (Biklen, 1995; Hoffman, 1981). Becoming a teacher also allowed many middle-class women to satiate their sense of adventure by traveling south to teach in the Freedom Schools after the Civil War or journey west to teach in newly established territories.

As female teachers were offered these new opportunities, they also encountered a number of obstacles. Discourses of morality surrounding the genre of early childhood education continued to position teachers as virtuous. Rules and regulations were imposed on their personal lives that reinforced this notion. Throughout the nineteenth century, female teachers were forbidden to ride in carriages with a man, frequent confectionery shops, or be out in public after 8:00 P.M. (Hoffman, 1981). Even into the twentieth century, women were legally required to resign their teaching positions once they married (Biklen, 1995; Hoffman, 1981).

Discourses of Science

Nay more: there are many who ought not to be educated, and who would be better in mind, body, and morals if they knew no school. (G. Stanley Hall, 1901)

Two decades before the turn of the century, rapid social, cultural, and economic changes continued to sweep through the United States of America. Waves of immigrants poured into northern urban areas from overseas as did a steady stream of free blacks searching for work and improved living conditions.

The publication of Darwin's *Origin of Species* radically changed beliefs about the nature of humans. "Darwin's book lessened faith in a fixed and knowable truth and put in its place thoughts of change, adaptation, development, and survival" (Weber, 1984, p. 47). Biological and evolutionary discoveries were applied to education, and Social Darwinism became embedded in a myriad of educational theories. Two distinct discourses emerged simultaneously and heavily impacted the field of early childhood education. These discourses were attached to two specific educational interest groups: the developmentalists and the social efficiency educators (Kliebard, 1986).

One of the most prominent leaders of the developmentalists was psychologist G. Stanley Hall. Hall drew on the work of Darwin to support his theory of child development and his scientific research methods of studying young children. Hall believed that each individual child passed through the stages of the cultural evolution of his or her race. "Ontogeny recapitulates phylogeny" became his proverbial phrase (Kliebard, 1986; Mohraz, 1979; Weber, 1984). According to Hall:

> The child relives the history of the race in his acts, just as the scores of rudimentary organs in his body tell the story of its evolution from the lower forms of animal life. . . . The all-

dominant, but of course mainly unconscious, will of the child is to relive this past, as if his early ancestors were struggling in his soul and body to make their influences felt and their voice heard. (Hall, 1904, in Kliebard, 1986, p. 45)

Discourses of race were blended with discourses of science to define intellectual potential. Hall argued that blacks as well as other "primitive races" should not be expected to perform at the level of their white counterparts, who were retracing the steps in their own development of a more advanced race (Mohraz, 1979). He argued against the notion that all children should be educated and advocated separate educational programs in order to meet the diverse needs of children.

Hall "scientifically" studied children by observing their behavior and using questionnaires that directly asked them about what they knew. He purported that through child study one could determine the needs and interests of children and plan curriculum accordingly. Hall encouraged the teachers of young children to observe behaviors and use questionnaires with each of the children in their care. Teachers could then meet the individual needs of each child.

Discourses of developmentalism gained more momentum as they became entwined with the discourses that were embedded in the social efficiency movement. Social efficiency educators drew upon the language of business and industry to develop new models of schooling. They were particularly interested in eliminating educational waste. Social efficiency educators argued that a child's education should directly relate to his/her future station in life. Providing a child with any amount of education beyond his/her future role was believed to be wasteful.

In order to determine the future roles of individual children, social efficiency educators such as Edward Thorndike turned to intelligence and achievement testing. Once tests identified the intellectual potential of students, differentiated curricula or special education programs were prescribed for the child. This allowed schools to mold and control "feebleminded" and delinquent students before they were "allowed to go out into life, [and] by the laws of heredity . . . inevitably pass on to future generations their defects and even diffuse them in the population as a whole" (Goddard, in Kliebard, 1986, p. 105).

Discourses of science merged with discourses of race and constructed blacks as genetically inferior in relation to their white counterparts. Further, large numbers of poor and immigrant students were also conceived as biologically inferior, based on their intelligence test scores. These students were removed from mainstream classes in schools and placed in domestic and manual training courses. One primary school in Philadelphia placed black and low-income children in courses that instructed them in "practical household economy, bodily cleanliness, orderliness, neatness, wise purchasing, 'sane decoration,' cooking, sewing and child hygiene" (Mohraz, 1979, p. 78).

Advocates of public school kindergartens appropriated the discourses of social efficiency to support their arguments for the merger of kindergartens with public grade schools. According to supporters, young children who were not attending kindergarten were missing the most valuable time for shaping the manipulative skills needed for manual training in the later grades. Consider the following assertion made by William Harris, a supporter of public school kindergartens:

> ... if school is to prepare especially for the arts and trades, it is the kindergarten which is to accomplish the object: for the training of the muscles—if it is to be a training for special skill of manipulation—must be begun in early youth. As age advances, it becomes more difficult to acquire new phases of manual dexterity ... (Harris, 1890, in Bloch, 1987, p. 38)

Discourses of morality, science, race, and class positioned teachers as the chosen ones (Kliebard, 1986). Teachers were believed to have the power to curb the antisocial tendencies of poor, immigrant, and black children. In 1901, Edward Ross, a leading sociologist, commented on the role of teachers in relation to the children and families with whom they worked:

> Another gain lies in the partial substitution of the teacher for the parent as the model upon which the child forms itself. Copy the child will, and the advantage of giving him his teacher instead of a father to imitate, is that the former is a picked person, while the latter is not. Childhood is, in fact, the heyday of personal influence. The position of the teacher gives him prestige, and the lad will take from him suggestions that the adult will accept only from rare and splendid personalities. (Ross, 1901, in Kliebard, 1986, p. 93)

While the role of the early childhood teacher continued to revolve around indoctrinating children of poor, immigrant, and minority families with middle-class values, it now also included identifying and preparing them for their future stations in life.

Discourses of gender interacted with discourses of science as early childhood teachers struggled to become validated as professionals. G. Stanley Hall's notions of science and his insistence that kindergartners collect scientific data on each child gave these women a sense of professional authority. The testing advocated by the social efficiency educators also moved female early childhood teachers into positions of authority as they administered standardized tests to children to measure their intellectual abilities (Finkelstein, 1988). By affiliating themselves with new scientific theories and innovations in curriculum and instruction, kindergarten professionals distanced themselves from other early childhood practitioners. Kindergarten teachers came to be viewed as more scientific and professional, and eventually kindergartens merged with public schools. Once connected to the elementary schools, kindergarten teachers received higher salaries and slightly higher status (Finkelstein, 1988; Spodek, 1988).

As kindergartens moved into elementary schools, the relationships were reconfigured between and among early childhood practitioners as were the relations between parents and kindergarten teachers. The notion that kindergarten teachers were holders of "expert knowledge" positioned them as professionals in relation to the families in their care. The distance between teachers and families who were not members of the dominant culture became greater.

As kindergartens moved into their new positions in the public schools, nursery schools were being established for middle-class children on campuses across the country. The nursery school, developed for the young children of needy families in England, was transplanted and rapidly took hold in the United States. Along with retaining the British goals of providing health and social welfare, the American nursery school incorporated the psychoanalytic theories of Sigmund Freud. Teachers of young children were trained to be concerned with a child's "natural impulses," "inner feelings," and "emotional stability" (Rothman, 1978). Teachers were advised to provide children with opportunities to play and be creative in order to meet the socioemotional needs of children. By the 1930s psychoanalysis became a field unto itself that focused exclusively on the emotional, unconscious, nonrational mind.

The majority of the nursery schools through the 1930s were private and catered to the middle class. Many were located in university-based laboratory settings which allowed researchers, psychologists, and others interested in child development and learning to observe children and generate new forms of "scientific" knowledge.

From the 1920s through the 1960s a discourse of behaviorism also emerged within the field of early childhood education. Drawing on Locke's notion of *tabula rasa,* that the child enters the world as a blank slate, early behaviorists, such as John B. Watson, contended that controlling the environment was the key to conditioning human behavior. In the words of Watson:

> The interest of the behaviorist in man's doings is more than the interest of the spectator—he wants to control man's reactions as physical scientist wants to control and manipulate other natural phenomena. It is the business of behavioristic psychology to be able to predict and to control human activity. (1925, p. 11)

In other words, behaviorism was defined as an objective science that focused on the conscious rather than the unconscious. B. F. Skinner, rising in prominence much later but building on the foundation of behaviorism laid by Watson, is probably best known for his work in the area of operant conditioning. Skinner's research with animals illustrated that desirable behaviors were repeated when they were positively reinforced and that undesirable behaviors decreased when the animals were punished. Child development researchers saw potential for the use of operant conditioning with children, and programs based on Skinnerian principles sprang into existence. In the early childhood classroom behaviorist principles were seen in the form of increased use of praise and small prizes or food for answering questions correctly or for the accurate completion of classroom assignments. The teaching machines, programs of behavior modification, and direct instructional strategies such as DISTAR that were seen in early childhood classrooms were also built on behaviorist principles.

Writing during the post-World War II era in which man was constructed as being free, open, and democratic, Skinner claimed that his work in behavioral psychology would help all Americans to reach this desired goal. At the same moment, these ideals were also being translated by educational leaders such as Gesell and, later, Piaget, who advocated a child-centered approach to teaching and learning. The child-centered approach of the 1960s, which was peppered with remnants of the theories of Rousseau, Pestalozzi, and Froebel, was embraced by early childhood educators as an alternative to the teacher-directed programs that were grounded in behaviorism. The newly emerging child-centered programs focused on catering to the needs, interests, and development of the individual child. Teachers, through facilitation rather than direct instruction, worked to unlock the inner potential of each child. Children were encouraged to become independent, self-reliant, and self-directed beings through play and discovery. Although the classroom environment was controlled by the teacher within those boundaries, children could choose what and how they wanted to learn.

Through the discourse of child-centeredness, the child is conceptualized as a unique individual being that possesses an inner potential. As children move towards reaching their inner potential, they are believed to experience set stages of development. Teachers are responsible for identifying the developmental stages that children experience as well as the needs and interests of each child in their care. Since it is believed that learning follows development, activities are presented to children at their levels of development across a variety of dimensions (e.g., social, emotional, cognitive).

Individuality as well as freedom is valued within the discourse of child-centeredness. In order to allow children to develop freely according to their own biological timetables, the role of the teacher is to facilitate learning rather than to teach children directly. As a facilitator, the early childhood teacher is responsible for assessing development and providing lessons and activities that meet each child's developmental needs and interests.

The discourse of child-centeredness contradictorily promoted emancipation and normalization (Burman, 1994). This discourse regulated teachers and children at the same moment as it promoted openness and democracy. Further, the discourse of child-centeredness was rooted in middle-class norms and values. Promotion of independence and choice was valued by white middle-class parents, while families from many nondominant cultural groups valued group work and cooperation. White middle-class children entered early childhood programs with an orientation to schooling that was quite different than that of their lower-income and minority counterparts. The normalizing discourse of child-centeredness positioned children and families who were not members of the middle class as lacking in intellectual potential.

The discourse of child-centeredness rose in prominence as the Civil Rights Movement was gaining momentum in the United States of America. Research findings reported that children did poorly in school because they lived in home environments that were culturally deficient (Bernstein, 1961; Bloom, Davis, & Hess, 1965; Hunt, 1961). The discourse of child-centeredness became entwined with discourses of race and class to position parents of low-income, working-class, and minority children as lacking in parenting skills and unable to care appropriately for their children materially or to stimulate them intellectually. Terms such as "culturally deprived," "culturally disadvantaged," and "culturally deficient" were attached to children and their families. A number of federally subsidized early childhood and parent education programs were developed during the administration of President Lyndon Johnson as he encouraged the nation to fight the "war on poverty." Parent education programs were organized to teach minority and lower-income parents middle-class ways of caring for and interacting with their young children. Parents were also encouraged to become involved with alternative early childhood programs such as Head Start.

Discourses of Developmentally Appropriate Practices

Teachers know that although schoolchildren can discriminate between fantasy and reality, their capacity for absorbing stimulation is limited. Teachers recognize signs of over stimulation such as when children become silly, overly excited, and carried away in chasing or wrestling; when children try to unduly scare others by relating dramatic accounts of events or experiences; when children are unable to calm down and focus on the activity at hand; or when they become preoccupied with a frightening event. Teachers' strategy is to prevent these behaviors rather than punishing them and to provide alternative calming activity. (Bredekamp, 1987)

The initiatives of the 1960s and 1970s, which had attempted to provide quality educational programming for large numbers of young children, encountered a conservative backlash in the 1980s. A renewed emphasis appeared on the testing and measurement of young children and the accountability of teachers. Fragments of discourses recycled from the social efficiency movement surrounded the entire educational community. The early childhood community, which has never been a unified body, argued over the issue of what was best for children. One group of educators advocated the infusion of more academically oriented instruction. They believed that the basic skills of reading, writing, and arithmetic should be introduced to young children in the context of early childhood programs. In opposition to this approach, another group of early childhood educators argued for maintaining a child development philosophy.

In the mid-1980s, the NAEYC was mobilized into action in an effort to stave off the increasing demands for academic instruction in early childhood programs. The NAEYC, after gathering information from early childhood educators all over the country, published a set of guidelines defining Developmentally Appropriate Practices (DAP) for programs serving children from birth to age eight (Bredekamp, 1987). The DAP guidelines are based on Piagetian theories of the child and child development. Developmentally appropriate practices are defined (in relation to inappropriate practices), and specifications are given for how they should be carried out by early childhood caregivers. The assumption is that all children in all classrooms will benefit from the same educational instruction. Discourses of race, class, and gender coalesce with discourses of developmentally appropriate practices to reify Eurocentric ideologies and promote them as best practices for everyone. A number of critiques written by scholars in the field of early childhood education (see, for example, edited texts by Kessler & Swadener, 1992, Mallory and New, 1994) emerged in response to the DAP publication. These scholars argued that the type of culturally specific standards advocated in the DAP guidelines maintain social inequities by hierarchically organizing knowledge and discouraging the development of alternative methods of teaching which may better meet the needs of nondominant groups of children (Lubeck, 1994; Mallory & New, 1994). NAEYC responded to the critique by publishing *Developmentally Appropriate Practice in Early Childhood Programs* (Bredekamp & Copple, 1997), a revised edition of the 1987 document.

The 1997 DAP document incorporates the work of theorists who place greater emphasis on the social aspects of a child's life. The work of Vygotsky (1978) asserts that children appropriate historically, socially, and culturally specific ways of thinking, speaking, and interacting from those contexts in which they live. Language is the bridge between the sociocultural context in which a child is situated and individual mental functioning. From this perspective, learning and development are both social and individual. Individuals absorb the thoughts and actions of those with whom they interact before they are able to use these "tools of the mind" (Vygotsky, 1978) in more personal ways. In other words, learning leads or happens in tandem with development.

If an individual's development depends on her/his interactions with others, then it is the role of the teacher to support and expand these cognitive functions that are already in the process of developing (Tharp & Gallimore, 1988; Berk & Winsler, 1995). Teachers provide students with experiences that are challenging for them yet can successfully be accomplished with the guidance of adults and more capable peers. The high priority given to language and the emphasis on co-construction of knowledge means that the most effective type of instruction would occur when teachers work individually with students or when students are placed in situations where they are provided with opportunities to collaborate. Parents, siblings, and other caregivers are called upon as resources to work in collaboration with school personnel.

Debate continues in the early childhood community over the issue of developmentally appropriate practices and what is best for young children. The revised document does integrate sociocultural theory with theories of child development. However, Piagetian theory remains the foundation upon which DAP is built.

The tensions that surround the genre of early childhood education highlighted in this chapter are evident within the Early Education Program (EEP) that is offered at Midwestern University. The EEP is the early childhood education program from which Ms. Nicholi, one of the two focal teachers, had been graduated.

CHAPTER THREE

An Early Childhood Teacher Education Program

As early as 1855 courses were offered through the School of Education for the preparation of high school teachers at Midwestern, but it wasn't until the 1950s that Midwestern offered course work for those who desired to teach elementary school. Responsibility for the preparation of educators of young children, rather than being assumed by the School of Education, evolved through the Department of Domestic Sciences, which later became the Department of Home Economics. In 1904, the Department of Home Economics offered prospective early childhood educators a major in household art. This major catered to young women and led to a career in either homemaking or early childhood education. The curriculum included courses offered by Midwestern's School of Education.

Over the decades, the support for and the physical location of the early childhood education program at Midwestern shifted with the national, political and economic climate. As the development of preschools and kindergartens swelled in the 1920s, the Department of Home Economics developed a Campus Nursery School. During World War II, as large numbers of women entered the workforce, Midwestern developed a statewide program with an emphasis on child development that was offered jointly through the School of Education and the Department of Home Economics. In the 1950s a child development major was offered through the School of Home Economics, while elementary education certification was offered through the School of Education. By the 1970s both the School of Education and Home Economics offered their own specific early childhood programs.

In the early 1980s national calls for educational reform reverberated throughout the education community. State departments of education became a more visible presence as their involvement in various reform efforts was heightened. In 1986, the state Department of Public Instruction issued new standards for licensing and certification. Three new elementary education programs were created within the Department of Curriculum and Instruction, one with an emphasis on grades one through six, a second with an emphasis on grades one through nine, and a third, the Early Education Program (EEP), with an emphasis on prekindergarten through grade three.

The EEP was a joint venture between the School of Family Resources and Consumer Studies, formerly the Department of Home Economics, and the School of Education. Half of the prospective teachers who entered the program would be enrolled in the Department of Child and Family Studies (CFS), which was located in School of Family Resources and Consumer Studies while the other half would be enrolled in the Department of Curriculum and Instruction (C&I) located within the School of Education. Graduates of the EEP are certified to teach children from birth through age eight. The first cohort of early childhood undergraduate students entered the EEP in 1991.

The Early Education Program

The EEP was described by the faculty and staff as "disparate," "conflicting," and "polyvocal." Dr. Laurie Reinke, an early childhood professor in C&I, described the multiple perspectives that she saw present in the program in the following way:

> There is a traditional early childhood perspective that's focused on issues of development, with everything tied back to notions of development. But within that there are two strands . . . there's a C&I version of it and a CFS version of it. So, there's a traditional kind of nursery school/home ec. perspective, and there's the kindergarten curriculum view of early childhood. And then, a third view that's woven . . . is a curriculum content focus. So literacy, math, and science as a template for understanding how you can keep these schools together, but it has a special version of that through C & I with its perspective in multiculturalism.

The multiple perspectives to which Dr. Reinke refers were visible both in interviews with faculty and staff and in the course syllabi and materials. The courses and the departments in which they are located are listed in Table 3.1.

Prospective teachers are required to complete five field placements as they move through the EEP. During the first semester prospective teachers spend two afternoons a week in a preschool setting and two afternoons a week in a kindergarten. Their field placements coincide with their methods courses. Prospective teachers spend their last two semesters teaching in a preschool setting and then either a grade 1–3 setting or kindergarten.

Faculty and instructors in the EEP highlighted four salient themes around which the program was built–development, diversity, thoughtful teaching, and

TABLE 3.1 Professional Sequence of Courses Taken in the Early Education Program

First Semester	Introduction to Education: Preschool through Middle School (C&I)
	Intellectual Development in Early Childhood and Its Relationship to Practice in Preschool Education (CFS)
	Social and Emotional Development of the Young Child in Early Childhood Education (CFS)
	Preschool Practicum (CFS)
	Kindergarten Practicum (C&I)
Second Semester	Teaching Reading (C&I)
	Teaching Language Arts (C&I)
	Practicum in Reading and Language Arts (C&I)
Third Semester	Concerns and Constraints in Teaching Young Children (C&I)
	Teaching Mathematics (C&I)
	Teaching Social Studies (C&I)
	Teaching Science (C&I)
	Practicum in Math, Science, Social Studies (C&I)
	Student Teaching: students can select to teach in elementary school or kindergarten (C&I)
Fourth Semester	Early Childhood Education Teaching Practicum (CFS)
	Preschool Student Teacher Seminar (CFS)
	Family and Community Influences on the Young Child (CFS)
Fifth Semester	Early Childhood Education (C&I)
	Seminar in Kindergarten through Middle School Teaching (C&I)
	Student Teaching: students select kindergarten or elementary school, whichever was not taken during the third semester

collaboration. As I began to look more carefully at how these themes were being promoted, I came to realize that individuals using the same terminology often meant completely different things. I found that these differing definitions occurred because department members drew on different discourses to describe their teaching philosophies, their course assignments, and their vision of what and who an early childhood teacher should be.

Although threads of many discourses could be detected in their conversations and course syllabi, two distinct discourses predominated—a discourse of child-centeredness and a critical, sociocultural discourse. The CFS faculty and staff members drew primarily upon the discourse of child-centeredness, and the C&I faculty and staff drew primarily on a critical, sociocultural discourse.

The notion that different discourses circumscribe the two departments can be traced back to their historical roots. The emergence of a discourse of child-centeredness in CFS can be linked to its roots in home economics and the development of Midwestern's laboratory preschool that promoted "scientific" child development knowledge. In contrast, the teacher educators in C&I, renowned for the critical perspective of their scholarly work, rejected the centrality of child development and, instead, drew heavily on a discourse of social reconstructionism.

Historically, social reconstructionists, such as Frank Lester Ward, and later, George S. Counts, promoted schools as vehicles for social change and social justice (Kliebard, 1986). They worked to create elementary and secondary school curricula that directly addressed social inequalities. The objective of such curricula was to shape children who would leave school with the knowledge and the desire to create a new social order. From this perspective, the child was viewed as being influenced by and having an influence on larger societal forces. The teacher was responsible for directly teaching children about social injustice.

Although a critical discourse was evident in the words and actions of the teacher educators in C&I, a sociocultural discourse was drawn upon as well. A critical sociocultural discourse carries with it a stronger critique of capitalism and American society than does the sociocultural discourse on its own. From within a critical sociocultural discourse, knowledge is viewed as being socially constructed and tied to the economic interests of those who are the most privileged in society. Schools are viewed as institutions that perpetuate the status quo and reproduce inequities (McLaren, 1989). Legitimating the experiences of all children, rather than simply the ones who are members of the dominant culture, and teaching children to question the social order are important goals of the early childhood teacher positioned within a critical sociocultural discourse.

Constructing Meanings of Development

The meaning of the four themes—development, diversity, thoughtful teaching, and collaboration—is constructed differently by members of the CFS and C&I faculty through their respective discourses. First, the term "development," which was loosely defined as the social, emotional, cognitive, and physical changes that young children experience as they grow, took on a very specific meaning when used within the discourse of child-centeredness that was drawn upon by members of the CFS faculty and staff. I turn first to Dr. Ellen Plumb, a senior faculty member, whose discourse and teaching practice typify those of her colleagues in CFS. The discourse of child-centeredness is evident in her talk as well as in the types of social practices in which she engages. The discourse of child-centeredness shapes the information that she conveys in class, the lessons and activities that she presents, the assessments that she uses to measure student performance, and her description of her own teaching practices.

For Dr. Plumb, a thorough understanding of development is the most important prerequisite for teaching young children. She said, "If you don't look at each child exactly where they are in their cognitive and language development and where they are in their social and emotional development and exactly where they are today, you're never going to teach them." She went on to explain that diagnosing levels of development was not an easy task for a teacher because each of the students in any given classroom is at a variety of developmental levels. One of the things that she works hard to get across to her students is the notion that each child is a unique individual. Dr. Plumb said, "That's what I would like to somehow incorporate at some level, the whole impact of this individual child today is unique and you as the teacher have the incredibly hard job of teaching 22 unique ones today."

Her course introduces prospective teachers to the stages of social and emotional development and moves sequentially through the stages of adolescence. Students are evaluated on their ability to identify developmental progression. Dr. Plumb describes her midterm examination:

> I have them read a book about a child from the Judy Blume books, any one of those they can read, and they have to go through this incredibly long list of diagnosing where the child is in development. Where are they in social development for each of the aspects we have studied theoretically, where are they in emotional development theoretically and empirically and then pull it together so that you understand. See we study all of those individual social support networks and all of that. How does all of that fit together to become the child you've read in the book?

Through this activity, Dr. Plumb involves prospective teachers in the act of measuring development. Development in this context is rooted in the individual child. For Dr. Plumb, it is the teacher's responsibility to identify accurately each individual's level of development before beginning to teach. Through such activities, students are engaged in learning experiences that are filtered through the discourse of child-centeredness, while simultaneously enacting practices that are embedded in the discourse. Dr. Plumb's students are immersed in the discourse of child-centeredness both as learners and as teachers. For example, Dr. Plumb explained how she teaches to the needs of her students:

> You've got to figure out where their "light" sort of is and you have to have something that's in common with them. They have to feel like you have something to offer that they need. And the trouble with teaching college is that they may not know that they need it. You may know they need it, but they're not going to learn it unless they know they need it.

The belief that learning cannot take place unless students are presented with information and materials that address where they are at in their various levels of development is as much a part of Dr. Plumb's approach to teaching adults as she wants it to be for those who are preparing to teach children. She views herself not as an instructor or teacher of her undergraduate students but rather as a facilitator of learning. In her words, "You know, none of us really teach anybody. We facilitate their learning and so if we need to help them come up with those thoughts, we need to just create situations." One implication of facilitating learning rather than directly teaching students is that educators must attempt to extract the knowledge that resides within the individual. As a result prospective teachers are never directly presented with information that challenges their thinking. Rather, information is presented that resonates with current levels of thought and what prospective teachers believe they need to know. Burman (1994) has identified two reasons why this approach to teacher education is problematic. First, through the discourse of child-centeredness, the ideas about children and teaching that prospective teachers hold when they enter the teacher education program are most likely the ones they will hold when they exit the program. Second, by being taught that they are to facilitate rather than teach, prospective teachers are left with little responsibility for the intellectual development of their students.

The topic of development, which plays a central role in CFS courses was not a focal point of any of the courses offered through C&I. Dr. Libby Braun, a senior faculty member in C&I, discussed her beliefs about development. She explained, "Developmental theories are images of what children do when certain skills develop at a point in time. And we know that there is tremendous variation and also social construction of those skills." Dr. Braun acknowledges that young children mature in some broad, fairly recognizable patterns of which teachers and caregivers need to be made aware but makes it quite clear that she considers stages of development to be social constructions rather than biological givens.

According to a critical sociocultural discourse, the social construction of development as being biologically rooted in the child privileges the white middle-class male child over children from nondominant cultural groups. Dr. Braun teaches a course focused specifically on early childhood education that encourages prospective teachers to interrogate the assumptions upon which various practices and programs incorporating issues of development have been built. Dr. Braun discusses her course:

> I emphasize history. I help students to understand the political, economic, gendered, language, raced, and cultural features that have gone into the history of the program. We also look at some of the ways in which our current programs are not just there as natural but are structured through the history of development, of policies and ideas about the program. Who it was to serve, who it wasn't to serve, the different goals for different groups of children.

By studying the historical contexts in which certain constructs have emerged, Dr. Braun helps prospective teachers understand that defining development as residing within the individual has benefited the dominant group in society throughout history.

Dr. Reinke likewise views development through a critical sociocultural discourse. She explains how being tied to the notion of development as a series of ages and stages could be a very limiting way to view children:

You either have an idea of what the first grade curriculum content should be.... You have to get through this part of the reading series or you have to get them to double-digit addition as dictated by the curriculum. Or you can look developmentally by what normal six-year-olds can do. You can be so intent on knowing what that map is that you don't pay attention to the scenery in front of you. You don't pay attention to those individual kids who come in who are placed all along the continuum of development. And they change from day to day and hour to hour. Those kids aren't just that little body there they're bringing with them a history and a set of connections with their family.

From Dr. Reinke's perspective, development is tied to one's family background and the social, economic, and political conditions in which each individual child lives and grows. In this context, development is presented as a social process as well as an individual one.

The critical sociocultural discourse that infiltrates Dr. Reinke's talk lives in the course that she offers to prospective early childhood teachers. Her goal is to help prospective teachers make connections between their practice and the societal forces that have shaped those practices. By examining issues such as development from multiple perspectives, prospective teachers are forced to examine their beliefs, how they have come to hold those beliefs, and how those beliefs affect the children and families with whom they work. This is done through the readings that are assigned and the activities that are presented to students. As an example, for a class session that focuses on the topic of developmentally appropriate practices, students are assigned readings that view developmental appropriateness through a Piagetian perspective, a neo-Piagetian perspective, and a Vygotskian perspective. After completing the readings, students engage in role-playing activities. According to Dr. Reinke, "they often get assigned positions that are contrary to what they hold so they have to look at both sides or actually very rarely just two sides. It's more often multiple sides."

Reinforcing the notion that development and learning occur through social interaction, Dr. Reinke organizes the course so that prospective teachers are continually engaged in the social practice of providing assistance for one another in order to learn class material or to complete course projects. For example, the "Semester Project" is a semester- long research project in which small groups of prospective teachers are asked to explore a topic of their choice from a variety of perspectives, then present their findings to the class.

Constructing Meanings of Diversity

The second major theme woven through the EEP is diversity. On a superficial level, faculty and staff use the term "diversity" to refer to the differences or variations between and among groups of individuals that included issues of race, class, gender, sexual orientation, religion, and physical ability. However, the meaning of diversity was much more complex when examined within the discourses that circumscribed the EEP.

Again, the words of Dr. Plumb serve as a representation of the views of the CFS faculty. Drawing on the discourse of child-centeredness, Dr. Plumb defined diversity as a set of individual characteristics that are unique to each child:

> You see, diversity is just another unique individual trait. If you just teach individuals, you don't have to have categories like diversity and special needs and creative and gifted . . . you don't need any of that. You don't need Chinese or Asian or any of that; you just need children.

From this perspective, race, class, and gender, like knowledge, are conceptualized as residing within the child. If the teacher is meeting the needs of her individual students, then she will automatically be addressing the issues of diversity that are part of that child as well.

Dr. Plumb teaches a course that emphasizes family and community influences on the lives of young children in which several projects and activities address issues of diversity from this perspective. The "Family Socioeconomic Problem-Solving Project" is a two-part project that is described in the syllabus as "complex." During Phase I of the project, small groups of prospective early childhood teachers are asked to work out a weekly schedule and a monthly and yearly budget for six different types of families. Students are presented with nine different family situations from which to choose their six family types. These include scenarios such as the following: "You are a sixteen-year-old never married female with a baby (thirteen months old). You did not complete high school"; "You are a twenty one-year-old never-married, female with a baby (eighteen months old) and a three-year-old. You completed high school in the lower third of your class"; "You are a twenty eight-year-old divorced male with children thirteen and seven who live with you. You manage a chain of fast-food restaurants."

Having chosen their six family types, the students must assign a socioeconomic status and race/ethnicity to each of the families. They are then asked to write a series of descriptions of the families, comparing the communities in Mayfield where they would be most likely to live. In the descriptions they are asked to:

> . . . describe how the family is affected by its ethnic and cultural group (e.g., will relatives be more or less likely to help with child care? Will family ties be stronger or weaker? Will extended family be more or less likely to help with expenses? Will strong customs direct certain types of life choices?).

In addition, students are asked to look at the history of the neighborhoods and compare the types of medical care, grocery stores, and schools that are available to these economically and racially diverse groups. Dr. Plumb asks them to determine if certain groups of people are "trapped by poverty in a neighborhood that is not contributing to their self-worth."

Through this activity, prospective teachers are forced to acknowledge the existence of racial and socioeconomic diversity. The project highlights the fact that socioeconomic status plays a large role in shaping the quality of the lives of the children and families with whom they will work. Race and socioeconomic status are looked at in the context of families and how the lives of the individuals within those families are affected. Although Dr. Plumb asks students to analyze the types of communities in which these families are able to live and the quality of the services that it would be possible for them to receive, she does not require that the analysis go beyond this level. Filtered through a discourse of child-centeredness, diversity is conceived as being located within children and families and outside of any sort of power relations. Dr. Plumb expresses what she hopes her students will take away from this project:

> What I want them to do is to understand the lives of those children that I know I've taught and I know that are out there. So that when they come in and say, "This child said this filthy word, ooh yuck!" then they know that the mother of that child may have had that child when she was fourteen. And I make them go visit schools so that they do know where the home, school, and community work together.

From Dr. Plumb's perspective, the problems that children experience in school are related to their family situations rather than to the institutional and social conditions that circumscribe schools. This project fails to acknowledge that social conditions arising from issues of racism, classism and sexism influence the lives of children and families but rather locates the social and emotional problems that young children may experience as being rooted within them or within their families.

By contrast within C&I race, class, gender, sexual orientation, etc., are conceived of as social constructs. From this perspective, simply being white, middle-class, heterosexual, and male privileges this dominant group of individuals over those groups who are raced, classed, and gendered differently. This privileging leads to differences in the way children are constructed in schools and has material consequences for their lives beyond the confines of the classroom.

Children from nondominant cultures who enter schools that promote the dominant culture often experience profound dissonance between the home and school (see, for example, Heath, 1983; Villegas, 1988). A critical sociocultural discourse acknowledges and values ways of thinking, learning, and acting that have arisen outside of the dominant culture. For example, consider the following statement of purpose extracted from the "Teaching Reading" syllabus:

> Reading is a complex social/cognitive process which children may learn with relative ease or with great anxiety. The purpose of this course is to help you understand your own expe-

riences with and attitudes toward reading and how those understandings inform your teaching. The course is also intended to help you understand the literacy in home and school contexts as it is learned and used by diverse children and adults. It is our goal to critically examine literacy teaching theories and practices that we believe promote all children's life long literacy development. An important emphasis throughout this course will be multicultural perspectives on current and past literacy education for young children.

Prospective teachers begin this reading course by examining their own assumptions and attitudes about literacy to help them to understand why they approach the teaching of reading as they do. The readings and activities are designed to help the future teachers develop a better understanding of how children from a variety of cultural backgrounds acquire literacy. The job of the teacher in this situation is to consider how power relations construct the child and to take these relations into consideration as curriculum is developed and instruction is carried out.

A critical sociocultural discourse also infiltrates the words and work of Ms. Jackie O'Connor, a graduate student and staff member in C&I. She spoke passionately about her work with prospective teachers in the area of diversity. Although she believes that it is important for prospective teachers to understand that issues of race, class, gender, sexual orientation, physical ability, and religious diversity construct children and families in very particular ways, she feels that it is crucial for prospective teachers to see how they are personally implicated in these relations of power. Ms. O'Connor explains:

> The most important thing that I want them to get out of the anti-bias stuff is that they're implicated in it. That they walk around living and breathing these biases and taking advantage of the privileges that they have and by being neutral and not addressing it, they're taking advantage of the privileges and affecting other people's lives. I want them to understand that they need to take personal responsibility in it. And that they can't be successful at teaching . . . they're not going to successfully teach an anti-bias, multicultural curriculum unless they deal with their own racism, sexism, and homophobia and all of those things at some level.

Ms. O'Connor works to help students understand that as teachers they are personally responsible for providing all of the children in their care with an education that allows each of them to be successful learners. Ms. O'Connor maintains that, in order to teach all children effectively, prospective teachers need to examine their own biases.

In the introductory early childhood education course that Ms. O'Connor teaches, activities are structured so that prospective teachers can work and learn together. By the time these students begin to study issues of diversity in depth, they have already built a classroom community that is based on mutual trust and sharing.

Within this community of learners, prospective teachers are encouraged to share their fears about addressing issues of diversity with children. Then, through readings such as *Anti-bias Curriculum: Tools for Empowering Young Children* (Derman-Sparks, 1989) and various articles contained in *Rethinking Schools* (Milwaukee, Wisconsin), published by educators who are committed to issues of social justice, prospective teachers are introduced to a variety of ways in which issues of diversity can be discussed with children as well as the many different strategies that are used for teaching diverse learners.

Constructing Meanings of Thoughtful Teaching

The third theme, thoughtful teaching, was used interchangeably with the term "reflective teaching" by members in CFS and C&I. Not surprisingly, however, "thoughtful" and "reflective" meant very different things when used within different discourses.

Dr. David Boetcher, a full-time staff member in CFS, talks at length about the student teaching seminar course that he facilitates and his role as a supervisor of student teachers. One of the main goals that he has for the prospective teachers in his seminar is to help them to become more thoughtful about their teaching:

> An appreciation for the thoughtfulness that goes into teaching is something that I place primary importance on. Putting a lump of play-doh down, a twelve-year-old can do that, a baby-sitter, my daughter can do that. She can be really excited with a group of two-year-olds, and observably it might not look much different than what a trained early childhood professional would do even some of her actions might be very similar. But, I want our folks to be thinking about what they are seeing. Not just that "Oh, these kids are busy or there aren't any fights."

Through a discourse of child-centeredness, Dr. Boetcher defines a thoughtful teacher as one who can observe a child or a group of children and make some meaningful interpretations about what it is that they are seeing. The ability to make such interpretations arises from the knowledge of children and child development that prospective teachers possess. Thoughtful prospective teachers, unlike untrained caregivers, are able to make connections among theory, practice, and what is being observed. Such thoughtfulness allows prospective teachers to monitor children's development and to ascertain their needs and interests as they change and grow.

In the student teaching seminar conducted by Dr. Boetcher, students are engaged in the practice of conducting thoughtful observations. When he is supervising their teaching, Dr. Boetcher often pulls student teachers aside and asks them to think through what they see. In his words, "Sometimes, I'll be able to grab them right there while I'm in the room. I'll just sit down at the table and say, what's going on over there?" Because Dr. Boetcher cannot be in the classrooms observing as often as he'd like, he requires each student teacher to carry a small notebook for recording observations throughout the day. At the end of the day, prospective teachers are asked to talk about their observations into a tape recorder. Prospective teachers share these tapes with Dr. Boetcher on a regular basis. He typically responds by posing questions that ask prospective teachers to think continually about the individual needs of each of the children in their care and whether their teaching practices are meeting those needs.

> My response would be something like, What did so and so learn from that interaction with you? What was in it for him or her? What was in it for you? What did you learn about the child from this interaction? And my goal is to get them to the point where they say, "Boy that was really ineffective," or "It worked but it wasn't good for this child," or "Wow! That's something I never thought about."

As prospective teachers begin to appropriate the type of questioning and the way of thinking about children that is advocated in their student teaching seminar, they are enacting what it means to be a thoughtful teacher from within the discourse of child-centeredness.

By contrast, in C&I the meaning of being thoughtful is very different. Within a critical sociocultural discourse, a thoughtful teacher is one who is able to recognize and articulate her own assumptions about children and teaching and to understand the perspectives of others as well. The C&I courses in the EEP are explicitly designed to provide prospective teachers with such abilities.

For Dr. Gerald Ray, a professor in C&I, a thoughtful teacher is one who has developed the ability to engage in critical self examination through the dissection of her own thinking:

> It is refreshing and exciting when people begin to clarify their own thinking on the issues and be mindful of what the reasoned conclusions are of people who disagree with them so that they do not arrogantly dismiss, lightly dismiss or ignorantly dismiss the conclusions of people who have reached different conclusions. I think that this is the principal purpose of this course. Now with that comes practice in slowly emerging skills in the dissection of one's own thinking. Now I could use fashionable language like reflection, reflective teaching. More concretely there are certain tools of reflection and self-examination; these are different tools. . . . If you can't recognize one of your own assumptions and critically analyze it then you are at a disadvantage in trying to solitarily, reflect on your practice. Certainly, you are at a disadvantage in terms of growth-evoking conversation about your practice with your colleagues. There is a vocabulary of unpacking ideas, considering them actively, playing with them, and challenging them that can lead to ongoing growth which, I am tempted to say, is essential.

Dr. Ray explains that the purpose of this course is to help prospective teachers clarify their own beliefs and to help them recognize that those who approach teaching from a different perspective also have viable reasons for believing and acting in the ways that they do. According to Dr. Ray, such critical thought cannot be generated solely by reflecting on one's own practice but rather occurs as the ideas of individuals come in contact with one another.

Dr. Ray attempts to teach prospective teachers how to be thoughtful through an "intellectual history framework." Prospective teachers study the work of educators of the past such as Plato or Rousseau and analyze the context from which their ideas emerged. From this historical perspective, prospective teachers are encouraged to make connections between past ideas and their present practices in an attempt to understand where their ideas have come from and why they believe the things that they do. After students have developed an understanding of their own assumptions, they are then challenged through various activities to understand why others believe as they do.

Whereas Dr. Ray's course is based on an historical perspective, Dr. Reinke's course focuses on the current political climate of the field. Dr. Reinke wants the students in her course to understand . . .

> . . . how the early childhood field is connected to areas that normally students never think of. They never think about how politics in Washington impact what happens to them. They don't think about how welfare reform might have an impact on them . . . the biggest goal I have is for them to see how their practice is situated in a lot of other contexts and they have to learn to identify what those contexts are, figure out what those contexts provide for them, and what they can give back to the contexts.

One semester-long assignment is to follow a newspaper reporter's account of a local school issue and then to analyze the coverage. This assignment helps prospective teachers explore how the media shape the political views of the audience. According to Dr. Reinke, students often complain about this activity and ask her why she can't just tell them what to do in the classroom. In her words:

> I've had people say, "You know, why don't you just tell me what to do?" And I just tell them, "I don't want teachers like that out there. We don't need sheep. We need people who think." And they need to learn to think if they're going to be good for themselves. One of the goals for the course is for them to be a good advocate . . . and in terms of good, I mean thoughtful . . . for themselves and young children.

Dr. Reinke defines a thoughtful teacher as one who can look beyond the face value of the information that is being presented and understand how the political motivations of groups of individuals shape the lives of teachers, children, and families in very specific ways. From this perspective teachers become responsible for looking at forces beyond themselves and analyzing how those forces shape and are shaped by their daily practices. By seeing multiple contexts interact with each other, prospective teachers come to realize that the choices they make in their classrooms have material consequences for themselves and the children and families with whom they work.

Constructing Meanings of Collaboration

The term "collaboration," the final theme highlighted by the teacher educators in the EEP, was used interchangeably with the phrase "working together." In CFS, through a discourse of child-centeredness, prospective teachers were encouraged to collaborate by sharing resources with one another and by working together on projects. For example, Dr. Plumb explained how prospective teachers could choose to work together on her final exam:

> And then the final exam is a team project if you want it to be. Those who are in the teaching major write a handbook for teachers on guidance telling why these aspects are important and how they play into theory. It helps them to work collegially, and they need to learn that if you work together with people it helps you.

From Dr. Plumb's perspective, working together helps to strengthen professional relationships among prospective teachers. Through a discourse of child-centeredness, prospective teachers, like the children they will soon teach, are conceived of as a group of individuals working towards personal goals rather than a collective group working towards a common goal.

The notion of collaboration in C&I directly connects to the educators' beliefs about thoughtful teachers. Both Dr. Reinke and Dr. Ray express the belief that thoughtful teachers can make a difference but stressed the fact that individual teachers cannot do so on their own. In the words of Dr. Reinke:

> I think more than anything, they should realize that they're not in this field by themselves. The early childhood field is a pretty dynamic place, and you can't do it by yourself. So what you have to do is to learn how to make connections with other people who can help you do your job, whether they're going to be resources in the classroom setting for you or a resource intellectually for you or emotionally. . . . [Teachers] are not going to be really powerful if they always work in their classroom by themselves. But if they know how to make connections, they can make a difference in individual children's lives. They can make a difference in classes in children's lives. They can make a difference in the profession.

For Dr. Reinke, creating supportive alliances with others in the field of early childhood education is an absolute necessity. These alliances can be forged within the classroom or school setting (e.g., parents or other teachers) or outside of the school context (e.g., in a local early childhood organization). Working together, teachers can make changes in their lives, the lives of children and their families, and the field of early childhood education itself.

Dr. Ray referred to his views on collaboration when he discussed the benefits of traveling through the EEP in cohorts. The cohorts were described by the faculty and staff as "forming personalities" and "creating their own energy." In some instances the "energy" that was contained within a cohort led to conflicts between prospective teachers and the EEP faculty and staff over the nature of assignments, the structure of the program, and various other issues. Consider Dr. Ray's discussion of the cohort groups:

> In a teacher education program, I think that the effort it makes to have kind of a cohort image has more benefits than drawbacks. I think that the drawbacks can be evident. It creates a socially volatile situation where the students get to know each other very well and they become emboldened and the leaders among them find their voice and that can be intimidating to people who are unaccustomed to being confronted by an angry mob or by a charismatic leader of an angry mob. But for all the discomfort that that might create for the lightening rods who have to endure it, I think there are long-term professional benefits to the students who go through that. There is a finding of professional voice. There's a discovery that one needn't be docile in the matrix of powerful social relationships. It is possible for them; it was possible for them, as members of a cohort in an inter-education program to complain, to suggest change, to criticize. And it would likewise be possible for them to do more of that than many teachers ever feel able to do once they get past the program and teach.

Speaking within a critical, sociocultural discourse, Dr. Ray explained that the cohort places students in a position where they can, if they choose, work collaboratively towards making changes within the EEP. Dr. Ray believes that, if prospective teachers realize the potential of working towards change within the program, this will translate beyond the EEP to schools and classrooms.

The Genre of the Early Education Program

The genre of the EEP provides prospective early childhood teachers with two fundamentally different ideologies from which to craft their teacher identities. Prospective teachers immersed in the genre of the EEP begin to appropriate the particular ways of speaking, thinking, and acting like an early childhood teacher that are available to them. Table 3.2 provides a brief summary of the distinct meanings within each discourse among the four major themes of the EEP. The table provides representative comments of the distinctive discourses used to discuss the themes.

TABLE 3.2 EEP Program Themes as Defined Within Distinct Discourses

Themes	Child-Centered Discourse	Critical Sociocultural Discourse
Development	"... if you can't look at each individual child exactly where they are in their cognitive and language development and where they are in their social and emotional development and exactly where they are today you're never going to teach them."	"Developmental theories are images of what children do when certain skills develop at a point in time. And we know that there is tremendous variation and also social construction of those skills."
Diversity	"You see, diversity is just another unique individual trait. If you just teach individuals, you don't have to have categories like diversity and special needs and creative and gifted . . . you don't need any of that. . . ."	"The most important thing that I want them to get out of the anti-bias stuff is that they're implicated in it . . . they're not going to successfully teach an antibias, multicultural curriculum unless they deal with their own racism, sexism, and homophobia and all of those things at some level."
Thoughtful Teaching	"An appreciation for the thoughtfulness that goes into teaching is something that I place primary importance on.... I want our folks to be thinking about what they are seeing. Not just that "Oh, these kids are busy or there aren't any fights."	"If you can't recognize one of your own assumptions and critically analyze it then you are at a disadvantage in trying to solitarily, reflect on your practice. Certainly, you are at a disadvantage in terms of growth-evoking conversation about your practice with your colleagues."
Collaboration	"And then the final exam is a team project if you want it to be.... It helps them to work colleagially and they need to learn that if you work together with people it helps you."	"I think more than anything, they should realize that they're not in this field by themselves . . . if they know how to make connections, they can make a difference in individual children's lives . . . in classes . . . in the profession."

As prospective teachers become immersed in the EEP they shape and are shaped by these discourses in very particular ways. These discourses influence how they think and act as teachers and define the parameters of their relationships with others. Table 3.3 illustrates the nature of the relations among the early childhood teacher and the children, families, and colleagues with whom she works within each distinct discourse. It is virtually impossible for prospective teachers to work outside of these two discourses as they are placed in student and teaching relationships, have their course work assessed, and are evaluated on their teaching techniques within either one or the other at any given time. The possibilities and constraints that surround the shaping of their own identities also grow out of how they are constructed within the genre of early childhood education as teachers of young children by the EEP faculty and staff.

TABLE 3.3 EEP Teacher in Relation to Children, Families, and Colleagues

Child-Centered Discourse	Critical Sociocultural Discourse
Teacher determines developmental level of each child and plans lessons and activities to meet the needs and interests of each individual child at their developmental level.	Teacher presents information that is in advance of a child's level of development yet is attainable with assistance from others.
Teacher addresses issues of diversity when they arise from the needs and interests of individual children.	Teacher presents curricula that directly address issues of diversity and provides children with strategies to help them work against prejudice and discrimination.
Teacher is continually monitoring the developmental levels of children and questioning how she can work better to meet the needs of individual children as well as her own.	Teacher is continually engaged in critical self-examination within a teaching collective.
Teacher builds colleagial relationships through sharing ideas and resources.	Teacher builds alliances with others to work towards social change.

Constructions of the Prospective Early Childhood Teacher

The teacher educators in the EEP describe their students as "competitive," "capable," "hardworking," and "very bright and interesting people." According to the three faculty members who had taught at Midwestern prior to the mid-1980s, this had not always been the case.

The early childhood program had been notorious for having some of the lowest grade-point averages on campus. Dr. Ray describes his perceptions when he began teaching at Midwestern in the mid-1970s:

> It was a child development preschool program and, to a lesser extent, preschool kindergarten program. They had perhaps the lowest, or certainly among the lowest, GPA requirements of majors on campus. And it was regularly abused by the football team and the hockey team as a place to put athletes who were in danger of having GPAs below NCAA requirements. And so there were people there with no interest in being educators, who were occupying the slots, taking up resources.

According to Dr. Ray, things changed when Dr. Plumb came to Midwestern and turned CFS around:

> She fearlessly closed the gap and enforced a minimum GPA. She tried to play hardball with the athletic department and it made a big difference. Those who didn't know how much she achieved by doing that couldn't underestimate how important a change that was.

However, despite the increased standards for admission, the EEP consistently filled last among the three elementary education programs. Dr. Ray attributes this phenomenon to the stigma associated with departments of home economics:

> Sexism can enter institutionally in terms of public attitudes towards appraisal of nursing or library science or teaching. It bites with particular vengeance on schools of home ec. and former schools of home ec. There is a reminiscence of that kind of thinking that makes schools of home ec, or whatever they've been subsequently called, among the lowest of prestige in parts of the universities.

Prospective teachers in the EEP, not unlike early childhood teachers across the nation, are described as being "young," "female," "white," and "middle class."

As faculty and staff members discursively construct the prospective teachers with whom they work, they draw on discourses of race, class, gender and the discourses of morality that are laced in and through the genre of early childhood education. These discourses combine with the academic history of the program at Midwestern to shape the way prospective teachers are constructed by the EEP faculty. Ms. O'Connor described the students with whom she works:

> So . . . you're twenty, twenty one . . . you've lived your whole life in this state, maybe in this town. You chose this profession because it's what good girls do . . . because you love kids. And you love your kindergarten teacher. And you want to have an apple on your desk. And you want to write on the chalkboard. . . . And you want people to like you and you want to have nice cute bulletin boards. And you want to shop at the Education Depot and . . . you love those things. You love crafts and you've always done well in school . . . you know how to be a good student . . . I always say to them, you're moving from being a student to being a teacher. That's what this program is all about. And students do things very differently than teachers do. Students don't take responsibility for things. They do what people tell them to do. Teachers take responsibility for things.

Dr. Reinke, herself a former kindergarten teacher, describes the prospective early childhood teachers in a similar manner:

> For the most part, they are overwhelmingly white and middle class from small towns around the country. They are teaching because they've always loved kids. . . . I usually have maybe one or two students that I would call intellectual.

The construction of the students in the EEP—"good girls," lovers of children, conformists, and not overly intellectual—conjures up very specific historical images of female educators of young children in the United States. The faculty description of contemporary prospective early childhood teachers parallels the types of early childhood educators Freidrich Froebel, Catherine Beecher, and others championed well over a century ago.

The identities of a prospective early childhood teacher are influenced by the discourses that circumscribe the teacher education program in which she has received her teacher preparation. However, there are influences beyond a teacher education program, such as the body of discourses that circulate in and through the elementary school context in which a teacher works, that shape her identities as well. The next chapter explores how teachers, students, and families are fashioned discursively at Woodlawn Elementary, the school in which Ms. Nicholi is a first-year teacher. After completing the EEP program and graduating in December, Ms. Nicholi was hired as an educational assistant at Woodlawn Elementary. She interviewed for a kindergarten magnet teaching position in the spring and was hired for the following academic year.

CHAPTER FOUR

Woodlawn Elementary School

The distance from Midwestern University to Woodlawn Elementary school is two to three miles. As I leave the university campus behind, I drive through an area in which restaurants, specialty shops, and small businesses are interspersed among residential areas. The scenery dramatically changes as I pass by the Mayfield Nature Preserve, which is less than a quarter of a mile from Woodlawn Elementary School. I turn right at the snow-covered sign marking the Wonago neighborhood and drive past the large Tudor, colonial, and Georgian-style homes that rest on spacious tree-filled lots. Nestled between the trees in the middle of the Wonago neighborhood stands Woodlawn Elementary, a large two-story red brick building built in the style of the 1970s. It is located on an expansive wooded lot. As I drive around to the back of the school, I notice a number of children sledding down a long, broad slope that leads to a wooded area of walking paths and a creek. Four playgrounds surround Woodlawn. Two of them are located in the back of the school, and several children are busily climbing, swinging, or sliding on the metal and plastic play structures.

The main entrance at Woodlawn is located on the second floor. Walking through the main doors, I am greeted by a black-and-white mural depicting a nature scene. I am struck by the low hum of noise emanating from the large open space. I had expected the noise level to be much higher in this school with its open design.

As I walk through the hall toward the steps leading down to the ground floor and Ms. Nicholi's kindergarten classroom, I am greeted by several staff members. The staff at Woodlawn is friendly and welcoming. Staff members speak highly of one another. It is common for teachers to share information with one another in their areas of expertise and to lean on each other for emotional support.

The staff is predominantly white, young, and female. Of thirty classroom teachers, two are white males and three (one male, two females) are people of color. The large support staff includes a social worker, a counselor, a school psychologist, an instructional resource person, reading recovery teachers, and others. The majority of educational assistants are African American females who travel among various classrooms to provide assistance to the teachers.

The staff often uses the word "unique" to describe the students and families at Woodlawn Elementary. This is intended to convey the wide range of diversity present there. Diversity, according to the prevailing discourse at Woodlawn, means differences in race, ethnicity, socioeconomic status, physical ableness, language, and geographic location. These children are drawn from five neighborhoods.

The school counselor, Mr. Jim Stone, provided me with some helpful information:

> Let's see, in sheer numbers we have around 500 kids. In this building that affects the culture of other things because we are crowded, and kids are put into situations where personal space can be a challenge. So in sheer numbers that can be difficult. Now that our numbers are dropping that has eased some. Diversity—we must have the widest range of socioeconomic groups here. I mean we have the poorest of the poor in town at Archer Avenue and also the most recently mobile. Many of the new families that come to town do find housing there or go to homeless shelters and then find a place on Archer. So we certainly have the newest of the poor, but also in the Wonago neighborhood around the school are some of the highest-income people in Mayfield proper.

Mr. Stone went on to describe the three other neighborhoods included in the Woodlawn attendance area. Cedar Bluffs was described as an area containing "middle-class little houses built right after World War II." Mr. Stone characterized the area as a "whole little subculture there of people pulling themselves up by their bootstraps." Adjacent to the Wonago neighborhood was another small pocket of families living in middle- and upper-middle-income-level homes. Mr. Stone compared the Archer Avenue neighborhood to the Warrensville Heights neighborhood which consisted of low-income African American families. He also described Archer Avenue as having a fairly large population of Asian immigrant families including Hmong, Cambodian, and Laotian.

Although children from five neighborhoods comprise the student body at Woodlawn, the staff often discusses the population in terms of only two neighborhoods: Archer Avenue and Wonago. A staff support person at Woodlawn acknowledged that children from other neighborhoods do attend Woodlawn but remarked that "We usually think of two neighborhoods: Wonago, being the neighborhood right around the school, and Archer Avenue." Children who were poor and of color were labeled "the Archer Avenue children," yet the poor white children who also lived in the Archer Avenue neighborhood were spared this label. Children of color from Archer Avenue were seen as "others" in relation to those children from the Wonago neighborhood who were white and middle class.

While the diverse make-up of the student body was described by the Woodlawn staff as "exciting," "wonderful," and "nice," this had not always been the case. Over the course of the past ten years, Woodlawn had gone through some major transitions. Change was a theme that ran through all of my conversations with the staff at Woodlawn.

Prior to 1988, Woodlawn Elementary had been the Wonago area neighborhood school. Woodlawn catered to the white middle- and upper-middle-class families that lived within walking distance. Numbers of students fluctuated between 200 and 300, and class sizes were moderate to small. In 1988, the Mayfield schools underwent some redistricting. New boundaries for school attendance were drawn, and the elementary-aged children from Archer Avenue were assigned to Woodlawn Elementary. Archer Avenue consists of a number of apartment complexes that are heavily populated with low-income families. The year following the arrival of the Archer Avenue children, it was also decided that Woodlawn would be a location for an English as a Second Language program because many of the families living in the Archer Avenue area were Southeast Asian and other non-English speakers. The English as a Second Language program drew children from other attendance areas in the city. Many of these children were also low income and in need of services such as free or reduced lunch and the breakfast program.

The number of children in poverty who entered Woodlawn during the early 1990s soared. By the mid-1990s, over 50 percent of the children served by Woodlawn Elementary were considered "high-needs." At any given time one third of the Woodlawn population was shifting either into or out of the school. According to Mr. Stone, this high level of mobility was indicative of the number of families at Woodlawn who were either homeless or living in transitional housing.

As the number of children in poverty grew, the number of middle- and upper-middle-class children plummeted. Parents from the Wonago neighborhood withdrew their children from Woodlawn and enrolled them in private schools. Moreover, many teachers who had taught at Woodlawn for years could not or chose not to work with this new population and left the school as well. Ms. Emily Greenspan, the social worker at Woodlawn, shared her perceptions of the situation:

> I think it was hardest on the teachers because they were pretty comfortable with the way they had taught before. Now they had to spend more time on classroom management kinds of issues and issues that we all assumed were being done at home . . . a lot of parenting issues and things that we assumed the parents were doing. But we were finding that, particularly with the lower-income kids, those things were not getting done at home. And so kids were needing breakfast, and they were needing to be worked with more about their behavior and things like that. So as the population changed, we had teachers who would leave and then we'd get new teachers in.

The teachers and parents were not the only ones leaving. In 1994 the principal at Woodlawn retired. Dr. Meredith Porter, who was formerly the principal at Apple Grove, an elementary school serving white middle- to upper-middle-class students and families, was hired as the new principal. Dr. Porter described the situation that she found at Woodlawn:

> When I came three years ago, it was chaos. You had people just desperate for things that worked. We had a community of parent groups that believed in public education that stayed. So it was an ideal situation. You come and people are going, "Help, help, help me. Help us do. . . ." At that time we only had two teachers who could actively say they didn't feel like they were failing. People were in tears every night. My office was full of behavior problems and angry parents.

Dr. Porter explained that parents and teachers were desperate for some teaching and support strategies that would work with the "high-needs" children that now populated Woodlawn. Because many of the teachers had left Woodlawn when its composition changed, Dr. Porter assumed the responsibility of hiring a new cadre of teachers who would be committed to the children in poverty at Woodlawn.

The group of white middle- to upper-middle-income parents who had kept their children at Woodlawn also made it clear to Dr. Porter that they were committed to working towards a quality education for all children. They wanted to be involved in the changes that were taking place at Woodlawn. Dr. Porter recalls what she was told at the first Parent Teacher Organization meeting she attended after she was hired: "Listen, we don't bake cookies here. It's a political action group."

According to Dr. Porter, this powerful group of parents worked with the Woodlawn staff to create a shared vision for a "progressive developmental multicultural program." They gathered statistics which illustrated that the children at Woodlawn had much higher needs than children at other elementary schools in the district that were receiving more funding. They collected literature that supported the idea of moving from grade-level classrooms to multiage classrooms in which teachers could team teach if they chose to do so. They made a case for more resource people to be hired. Once compiled, all of this information was taken to the administration and presented at a school board meeting. Consequently, the school board reversed its earlier funding decisions in favor of Woodlawn. Class sizes were reduced; funding for support staff was increased; walls were knocked out in order to enlarge classrooms for team teaching, and summer institutes were funded so that teachers could learn how to instruct and design multiage curricula.

Dr. Porter further reported that, just as the new developmental multicultural program was getting off the ground last year, Woodlawn was faced with another redistricting plan. The district decided that the percentage of high-needs children at Woodlawn was excessive. Boundaries again shifted, and the Archer

Avenue children were spread out across three elementary schools. However, the other two schools to which the Archer Avenue children were to be sent did not have the space available for full-day kindergarten, which the district felt was necessary to provide. As a result, Woodlawn was designated as the site for a kindergarten magnet program.

The kindergarten magnet program called for 40 percent of the children to be drawn from the Archer Avenue neighborhood and 60 percent to be bused in from other attendance areas. Plans for locating five kindergarten magnet classrooms at Woodlawn moved ahead while supplies and classroom resources were purchased.

All of this preparation was thrown into disarray at a board meeting a few weeks later, at which it was decided that any school that wanted a full-day kindergarten would be funded. Understandably, parents who had planned on enrolling their children in the kindergarten magnet program at Woodlawn now enrolled their children in their neighborhood schools instead. The kindergarten magnets, originally intended to be balanced, were now filled with large numbers of children considered to be high needs. In the words of Dr. Porter:

> So the decisions weren't timely and they weren't made together. What did happen is that we didn't get enough people on the other side of the magnet. They had to pull the teachers and the classes became 75 percent to 70 percent high-needs.

Currently the number of children in poverty attending the four full-day kindergarten classes which comprise the magnet program is still very high. Dr. Porter considered the kindergarten magnet program to be "a school within a school." It was not part of the progressive multiaged developmental programming. She explained however that "the teachers were hired with the same philosophy and team teach with our teachers, yet the kids are not multiaged and are much higher-needs than our regular school population."

The "regular school" to which Dr. Porter refers is comprised of the children who are enrolled in the kindergarten/first grade through fourth/fifth grade multiaged classrooms. The relocation of the Archer Avenue children in grades one through five has decreased the percentage of children receiving free and reduced lunch, and the mobility factor is much lower as well. The problem of large numbers of Archer Avenue children moving in and out has also been minimized this year due to the redistricting. For the time being, Woodlawn is accepting only the younger siblings of the Archer Avenue children who are currently enrolled in grades one through five. The staff members at Woodlawn articulated that the smaller population of children coming from Archer Avenue made classes more manageable and reported that things were running more smoothly this year.

Several faculty members were critical of the way that the district had relocated the Archer Avenue children over the years. As one staff member said, "If Archer Avenue were any other middle-class white neighborhood, it [the redistricting] wouldn't have happened." Terms such as "dilute" and "dispersal" were used by other staff members as they discussed how the district dealt with the Archer Avenue population. One staff member explained that the children of the Archer Avenue neighborhood were placed in nine different schools:

> They began to bring Archer Avenue here because Grant and Mayfair couldn't hold any more. But I'm not sure what all the politics were. I'm sure Archer is the only neighborhood in the city where the children attend nine different schools. You've got three elementary schools and then you've got four middle schools and two high schools. Who is advocating for our friends in poverty? It is a population to be dispersed.

Many of the staff members at Woodlawn discuss issues of power at the school district level and lament how the power structure works in favor of those families who are white and middle class. They recognize that the continual relocation of the Archer Avenue children is not an educationally sound practice and that it would not be permitted to happen to any of the white middle-class children in Mayfield. Yet, this critique of power never translates to Woodlawn. The staff never discusses the power structure at their own school nor its effect on the families and children with whom they work. Instead, the discourses of morality, race, and class that Woodlawn staff members draw upon position the Archer Avenue children and families as deficient in comparison with their white middle-class counterparts. Much time and effort at Woodlawn is geared towards inculcating white middle-class ways in the Archer Avenue children, especially those who are African American.

Shaping the Identities of Children

Every staff member with whom I spoke used the term "high-needs" to describe the population at Woodlawn. Although eligibility for free and reduced lunch and mobility were the official indicators of high-needs at Woodlawn, unofficially the term was used to identify a child from a nondominant culture who has not yet been socialized to white middle-class ways of thinking and acting. High-needs translated into inappropriate behaviors that needed to be curbed through very structured activities and strict discipline. When I asked a teacher of one of the kindergartens in the magnet program to explain what she meant by the use of the term "high-needs," she chose her words carefully:

> I mean we've come to a consensus that we don't put a lower expectation on the kids because of the their economic level–I mean Carly who sits right here doesn't have crayons at home. She doesn't have pencils or crayons. They've had–I don't like to use the term culturally deprived–they have certainly had important experiences in their lives. It's shaped them . . . but a lot of them have never had school experiences. So whenever we can, we bring their culture into the classroom. But when you have kids who have come from

lower–income families, we generally assume that they're going to need more resources and more help, but that's not always true. . . . It's really easy to say that every kid who comes from Archer Avenue is going to be low skilled and have behavioral problems, but that's just not true. It's a catch-all term that just describes the kids who live in poverty.

Although this teacher claims to reject the notion that all of the Archer Avenue children have poor skills and behavior problems, the assumption that many of them do surfaces in her words. For her, high-needs children are economically and culturally disadvantaged, nonwhite, come to school without the experiences that middle-class children bring, and are often low skilled and/or have behavioral problems.

Another kindergarten magnet teacher focuses on behavioral issues when she describes how she structures her practice in order to meet the needs of high-needs children:

> From what I've seen in my class specifically . . . it's got to be structured–not a lot of freedom but yet some freedom for them. A lot of structure, a lot of discipline things, and yet to love them too. That's a biggy!

She describes the make-up of her kindergarten class in the following manner:

> I have a very diverse population: a little boy from Czechoslovakia, three Hmong children, one from Sudan . . . hmm. . . . I have Charlie, who is American–he comes from the Rapid Falls area–and the rest are African American. It's a very interesting group of kids.

Although at first glance it may be difficult to identify to whom she is referring as the high-needs children in her class, at Woodlawn the description of Charlie as a Rapid Falls child signifies that he is in a category separate from the others. The west side neighborhood from which Charlie is bused is predominantly white, comprised of middle- to upper-middle-income residential areas. It is interesting to note how this teacher makes a distinction between Charlie's American nationality and the children of African American descent. Clearly, she sees Charlie as the only American child in her class. White middle-class, American-born Charlie is an example of the type of child to whom Woodlawn staff members refer as a "role model."

I first heard the term "role model" as it was used to describe the children from the Wonago neighborhood and those children who were bused in from white middle-class areas to attend the kindergarten magnet program. This usage of the term indicated that the staff at Woodlawn expected the high-needs children from the Archer Avenue area to adopt the behaviors and actions of the white middle-class children. Although she seemed uncomfortable using the term, Ms. Greenspan did so nonetheless:

> So the Gold and Gray buses bring kids from Rapid Falls, Coventry, and Apple Grove. Those kids all come because their parents wanted them in all-day kindergarten programs

for various reasons. And they're—I don't want to say that they're role models but—you know—they are.

Ms. Nicholi also used the term "role model" when she discussed how she was asked about her preferences for students. Several new children had moved into the area and were to be assigned spots in the kindergarten magnet classrooms. Ms. Nicholi said, "I was asked if I wanted one Archer Avenue child or two role models. I told them I'd take the Archer Avenue child." This question further exemplifies the attitudes that are held by the administration and the teachers who work at Woodlawn. The idea that two white middle-class children would be less challenging to teach than one child who is in poverty and a member of a nondominant culture illustrates just how firmly entrenched racist and classist notions are embedded in the discourse. A discourse of normalization (Popkewitz, 1993) constructs those children who are white and middle class as "normal" and those children from the Archer Avenue area as "not normal." What constitutes "normal" at Woodlawn is a set of "appropriate behaviors" that have been sanctioned by the school.

Time and again I was told by faculty at Woodlawn that the Archer Avenue children exhibited inappropriate school behaviors. For many of the Archer Avenue children, kindergarten at Woodlawn was not their first school experience. Many of them had attended the Head Start program located in their neighborhood. However, in the eyes of the Woodlawn staff, this was discounted as an educational experience. According to Ms. Nicholi, the Head Start program "had no expectations for the children—no writing, no academics." Ms. Nicholi described it as being a "play experience." She reported that on several occasions teachers from Woodlawn had called the Head Start center to ask about some of the academic and behavioral problems that the Archer Avenue children were experiencing in their classrooms only to be told that "the children hadn't experienced any problems at the Center." According to Ms. Nicholi, the children had not experienced any problems in Head Start because the teachers "had no expectations for the children."

At Woodlawn, "appropriate behaviors" were defined on both an individual and a social level. On an individual level, "appropriate behaviors" were exhibited by children who were able to regulate their own actions. For example, following directions, walking in a line, and speaking in a quiet voice while in school. On a social level, "appropriate behaviors" were those which showed that the children were able to cooperate with others. These interactions included sharing materials, solving problems through discussion rather than the use of force, and being able to take turns with others in games and activities.

Rather than attributing the lack of socialization to the lack of a more formal academic school experience, the staff at Woodlawn often attributed what they saw as "inappropriate behaviors" to the poor parenting skills of the Archer Avenue parents. Mr. Stone lamented that many of the children in the kindergarten magnets came to school without "a whole lot of experience before kindergarten in sitting and paying attention." He went on to explain:

> . . . you would hope that they have had some experience sitting and being able to sit for ten or fifteen minutes at a time and pay attention, whether that was an experience that they had maybe at their church or at home, other than sitting watching TV, or even some experience with adult directions: "I need you to sit here and this is what we're going to do for the next 10–15 minutes." You hope for the kids to be able to do that impulse control thing.

A discourse of normalization permeates Mr. Stone's words as he makes assumptions about the home lives of the Archer Avenue children. He does not acknowledge that sitting quietly for fifteen minutes and paying attention for sustained periods of time are skills that many white middle-class children bring with them from preschool into kindergarten. At Woodlawn there is no allowance for any other type of behavior. Indeed, the staff discusses the Archer Avenue children, not as being socialized differently but rather as not being socialized at all.

However, those Archer Avenue children who had attended kindergarten at Woodlawn and had successfully been inculcated with white middle-class ways of behaving in the classroom were also referred to as role models for the entering kindergartners. Again, the term "role models" was used to signify appropriate behaviors. In the words of Dr. Porter:

> When we get high-needs kindergartens in the magnets, we get a lot of those kids who don't socialize, who have had no schooling. Their behaviors are very difficult, very demanding. Now you have a classroom with just half the kids who are new to school, new to rules, new to somebody telling them proper school type behaviors. So you decrease your behavior issues. Plus you have the role model. You have the older kids . . . sit on the rug. They'd go sit on the rug. You could pair them up. You have a built-in team teaching situation with students.

In subsequent conversations Dr. Porter made it clear that the multiage classrooms in kindergarten through fifth grade had been adopted not for academic purposes but rather for behavior management. While the multiage classrooms provided one mechanism of social control, the strong school-wide emphasis on discipline at Woodlawn provided another.

The problem of maintaining discipline at Woodlawn was described as "gigantic." I was told that there were so many disciplinary infractions during any given day that it took five people on a rotating basis to deal with all of them. Dr. Porter and four other administrative staff members wrote up discipline referrals, spoke with children, and met with parents. The African American children from the

Archer Avenue neighborhood were constructed as the primary source of behavior problems.

The Woodlawn Learning Center, WLC as it was often called, was a room to which children were sent by the teacher when she felt that they needed to be removed for a short period of time from their regular class. It was a place where many of the Archer Avenue children, especially boys, spent a substantial portion of their time. Although most of the teachers sent children down to the WLC as punishment for misbehavior, the African American woman who ran it saw its purpose differently. She fed the children who were sent to her when they were hungry and allowed them to rest if they were tired. When I asked her about her job, she described it to me in the following way:

> I do many things here. I'm an educational assistant, but I also help in discipline. And what I mean by discipline is that my part is not really dealing with making decisions on what to do with a kid. That's not my job. A lot of our kids that we have here, the African American kids I mean, sometimes they come in not feeling very well and not having enough sleep or they didn't have enough breakfast or whatever and they're not able to learn. Some kids feel like it's a privilege to be down there because you can have a good day and it's like, "Wow! I get to go down there and talk with Tina and have some breakfast or have lunch." Some kids don't like it because it's a disciplinary part for them. They know that they can't take the time out in the classroom, so this is where they need to come and take the time out. They have to sit quietly in order to get their thoughts together and then they have to have a plan before they can go back to class on "How can I get back in the class? What do I need to do to stay in the classroom?"

Behavior problems that were considered more serious than simply needing a time out in the WLC were dealt with more severely. It was not uncommon for children, even kindergartners, to be suspended from school for physically harming others, destroying school property, or behaving in a violent manner. The staff members at Woodlawn used the word "suspension" to describe the removal of a child from the school for a period of a day or more. But, when I asked for clarification, I was quickly assured that these "were not really suspensions." Mr. Stone, who described his job as being 20–30 percent handling discipline, described the kindergarten suspensions in the following way:

> A variety of kids in the K-magnet classes this year come to kindergarten without a whole lot of experience in sitting, paying attention, all those basic skills that you hope they have a little bit of when they first hit kindergarten. Some of the same kids are currently in situations at home that are loud sometimes, chaotic sometimes, unsupervised sometimes. So now we get back to K-magnet here. More than one or two kids have been violent in a big way–throwing tantrums, seriously hurting other kids, seriously hurting staff members, kicking, biting, that kind of stuff. . . . Well, we've used "time outs" on rare occasions. We've sent kindergartners home with a message like: "Mom, nobody can be here if they are going to hit the teacher. So he needs to go home and think about that for a day, and you need to come back tomorrow morning to meet with the principal."

After a child has been suspended from school, he or she is driven home by a staff member. The parents are told to schedule a meeting and bring the child back the next day. In essence the school forces the parents to take responsibility for the child by not allowing the offender to return to school until a parent, the child, and Woodlawn staff members have met to discuss the problem. Ms. Greenspan, who is also involved in disciplinary issues, explained how this part of the process works:

> What we do when we suspend a kid is ask them to stay home a day and they must always come back with their parent. So some of those suspensions from Anne's room were not really suspensions. We just took them home and said, "Really, we're so concerned that you can't come back without your mother." Because we really feel that moms are the key here to making it work. And often moms don't want to come in, but if you keep them home until the mom can bring them back, then she is pretty much forced to come in.

A substantial number of children in the Archer Avenue neighborhood are being reared by single mothers. The economic hardships they face on a daily basis force many of them into low-paying jobs outside of the home. Yet the talk at Woodlawn cast the Archer Avenue mothers as shirking responsibility for their children. Such a construction can be traced back to the discourses of domesticity that emerged during the 1800s which placed mothers in the home as nurturers of young children and as those who were responsible for holding the family together. The Archer Avenue mothers do not fit into the role of the nurturing mother embedded in this discourse and were consequently criticized by the staff.

Only one faculty member, a kindergarten teacher, mentioned the role that fathers play in the lives of the Archer Avenue children. She felt that the presence of a father in the family made a huge difference to children both in terms of their cognitive level and their level of maturity:

> You know a lot of kids who live in poverty live in a single-parent family, and I have found that in this class there are a lot of dads at home. That's pretty new for me. In some cases it's not always the best situation, but just in terms of the personality that creates in the kids, I mean, it's interesting. And when the dad is involved, especially with the boys, their skills are a lot higher. They're more mature.

From her perspective, children who live in a two-parent family are better off than those who live just with a mother even if the circumstances aren't the best.

Discourses of gender, morality, and Romanticism became intertwined as Mr. Stone constructed the kindergarten teacher as a gentle, loving, "surrogate mother" in relation to the Archer Avenue children.

> The teacher, the kindergarten teacher to me is the person who has, by far, the most influence with the children because she becomes like a surrogate mother. They become so bonded to her. I mean in most schools, kindergarten discipline has never gone beyond the

> classroom because the teacher loves them to death and also has that leverage with them when they act up, to help them take a little look at their behavior. That same teacher can build a good bridge with the parent and when the kid sees that bridge there is even more leverage . . . but here it goes beyond the classroom now because of several things. We've had some kindergartners here whose behavior has been so outrageous that the teacher wouldn't be comfortable dealing with it in their classroom.

According to Mr. Stone, although the kindergarten teachers possess these nurturing characteristics, they still have difficulty dealing effectively with the Archer Avenue children whom he constructs here as being uncontrollable. In fact, one white female kindergarten magnet teacher had left abruptly after two months owing to her inability to deal with the children. Ms. Barbara Grimke had been hired in October to replace her.

The discourse that the staff at Woodlawn draws upon locates inappropriate behaviors within children and their families. There is very little discussion about how the school itself or other external forces may be implicated in producing these negative actions or reactions in children. Behavior problems at Woodlawn are almost always discussed as arising from individual children who were overwhelmingly African American and poor.

A Map of Behavior: The Kindergarten Report Card

The emphasis on behavior was also exhibited in the types of curriculum and instruction that were presented to young children. Since the kindergarten magnet program was new, the magnet teachers had created their own kindergarten curriculum. I was directed to the kindergarten magnet report card by the kindergarten teachers for a better understanding of their objectives for the program. They had worked from the kindergarten/first grade multiage report card but had modified it to meet the needs of the kindergarten children in their classes. The skills and concepts that the magnet teachers presented to the kindergartners throughout the year were designed to meet these objectives.

Fifteen of the forty-six objectives (33 percent) of the kindergarten magnet report card directly address issues of behavior. These fall under the heading "Personal, Social, and Work Skills" and are prominently displayed on the first page of the three-page report card. Items listed under this heading include "shows self-control," "follows directions from all adults at school," "keeps hands and body to self," "demonstrates good listening habits," and "works for an appropriate amount of time on task at hand."

The kindergarten/first grade multiage report card is similar to the kindergarten magnet report card but consists of seventy-nine objectives. The objectives emphasize the advanced academic skills that older children are expected to master but still include twenty objectives (25 percent) that focus on behavior.

The staff at Woodlawn has adopted the concept of multiage classrooms primarily for the purpose of behavior management. In the multiage classrooms children work with the same teacher or team of teachers for a period of two years. Some teachers work in pairs to teach classes of 40 or more children. Other teachers retain their own individual classrooms but plan curriculum together and occasionally work with different combinations of children across two "home rooms." The kindergarten magnets are the only four classes in the school that are not specifically multiage classes.

Experimentation with a developmental curriculum had begun at Woodlawn prior to the creation of multiage classrooms. According to Dr. Porter, the disparity between children's levels of development in any given classroom had become so great that the teachers were no longer able to teach to a specific grade level. Dr. Porter described the frustration that teachers had shared with her:

> "In my second grade class there are 23 kids. Eleven of them cannot read. Five of them are reading at eighth-grade level, and four or whatever is left are at grade level." And you'd say, "Wow! At Apple Grove I might have one kid who couldn't read and they were in a special ed. program." So I had to say to these people, "You're not teaching second grade. Why do you think you're teaching second grade? Do you leave the kids who don't read there?" And they go, "No, we work with them. We teach them how to read." "Okay, so get out of this thought that you're teaching second grade."

Teachers were encouraged at that time to move from the grade-level curricula that were so familiar to them and to begin teaching the children based on their individual levels of development.

The curriculum was described as "developmental" in the sense that it was individualized for each child. Children were not placed in specific grades. Rather, at the beginning of the academic year each child was assessed in order to identify her/his developmental level. Ideally, once a child's level of development had been identified, teachers and parents would discuss the goal for that child's progress over the course of the academic year. Children received instruction based on their developmental needs in a variety of areas. Dr. Porter explained this further:

> Academically, because the school is so developmental, they are certainly not slotted into a grade level. So if you're a bright, talented child—because we have to open up our curriculum to get the lowest end, we also have to open it up to make it hit its highest end.

Teachers at Woodlawn discussed children and their needs in terms of development. Yet, individual ability and achievement were almost always described in terms of grade level. Children were referred to as being "above grade level," "at grade level," or "below grade level." The faculty at Woodlawn expressed a collective goal of working to get every child "up to grade level." Even the multiage classrooms were referred to in terms of grade level: "the kindergarten/first multiage classroom."

All the teachers at Woodlawn discussed at length the teaching methods and strategies they used in attempting to meet the developmental needs of the children. The teachers with whom I spoke appropriated the discourse of child-centeredness. Terms such as "needs," "readiness," and "developmentally appropriate" were sprinkled throughout their conversation. Consider the following kindergarten teacher's comments as she discusses her attempt to meet the diverse needs of her students:

> Well, in a school like this, upper classes are multiage classes regardless of whether you have a K/1 or a 2/3 or a straight kindergarten because the kids come from so many different levels. I mean I have kids who can read at third grade level . . . and then I have Latisha, who is still trying to learn the letters in her name. So there's no curriculum guide where you can just look and say the kids need to know this and this and this because some of them are already way beyond that or some are way below that. So I teach based on the needs of my kids. I look at where they're at. I try to take notes and through observation and talking with parents I see where they are at. I take them to the next level.

All of the kindergarten teachers discussed their desire for more unstructured, hands-on, playful activities that would allow children to make more choices about their learning, yet they believed that the behavior of the children often stood in their way. One teacher articulated that she felt the most comfortable when she was doing whole group instruction with her children yet really wanted to do more learning center types of activities. She had tried to involve her class in learning centers one day, but "the children had a real rough time of it." She believed that the children's lack of self-discipline prevented them from making choices about their learning and following through with those choices.

Each of the teachers grappled with how to provide children with choices while simultaneously controlling their behaviors. More importantly, these teachers felt that it was their responsibility to make certain that each of the children in their care learned the academic material that they needed to know as they left their current educational setting and moved on. Terms such as "basic skills," "teacher directed," and "drill and practice" were used by teachers as they described the academically-oriented nature of their practice. One kindergarten/first grade multiage classroom teacher talked about how she managed to move between being teacher directed and child centered:

> I don't have any magic formula for kids, but I do think that children need a certain structure, and they need to know what their limitations are. And they need to know where that line is and what happens when they cross it. And they need to know that you're going to care about helping them to stay within those bounds and to have a good day within those bounds and to feel good about themselves and that there are consequences for choices and behavior. I like to allow kids to have choices in their learning. I think kids should be able to do that. So part of the day is teacher directed, but much of the day children have choices as to whether they want to extend themselves.

This teacher scheduled a "structured" choice time in her classroom for the last 45 minutes of each morning. She referred to this choice time as "planning centers" explaining, "We call it 'planning centers' because the children actually write a plan about where they're going and what they're going to do. It's kind of a High Scope plan-do-review." Before children could visit any of the learning centers, they had to write a plan that designated where they were going to go over the span of the 45 minutes, and they were responsible for sticking to it. According to her this plan helped children "think about what they are going to do" and "stay committed to finish something before they move onto something else." She also contended that it gave them another opportunity to practice reading and writing.

There was tension in one kindergarten teacher's voice as she noted that some of the children in her class, especially those from Archer Avenue, were not responding to learning activities that were considered developmentally appropriate and that she had turned to more academically oriented instruction:

> ... with a lot of kids I don't feel like I can be developmentally appropriate with them because they can't wait. Next year they're going to go to a new school, and nobody's going to know them. I don't know; I need to try everything possible to see if it works because I don't want them labeled LD or put in remedial reading. I want them to have basic skills so that they don't have to suffer through that.

For this teacher teaching basic skills meant what she referred to as "drill and practice."

The teachers at Woodlawn seemed to wrestle with their notions about teaching young children. On the one hand each teacher expressed her desire to become more child centered yet believed that, because of their behaviors, the children could not handle the increased academic freedom. On the other hand, the teachers at Woodlawn embraced a highly teacher-directed, skills-based curriculum which they felt better met the needs of their Archer Avenue children. This type of learning environment helped to keep behaviors in check, and teachers also felt that the children responded better to being taught basic skills in reading, writing, and mathematics.

Celebrating Diversity

Multicultural education, a theme that emerged in my discussions with Woodlawn administrators and support staff, was almost entirely absent in my discussions with classroom teachers.

Dr. Porter admitted that multicultural education was difficult for her, being a "little white woman from the Midwest." Diversity was not something that had been a part of her life before coming to Woodlawn. She explained that course work and her experiences at Woodlawn had developed a sensitivity in her which caused her to look more carefully at how particular children were being represented in school. She asked questions such as: "When you read, who are you reading about? Who are you teaching to? And when you sing, who are you singing about? Which cultures are you representing?" She stated that Woodlawn "had a long way to go" in the area of multicultural education.

Many activities sponsored by the school supported the notion of celebrating diversity through a "tourist approach" (Derman-Sparks, 1989). The term "tourist approach" refers to the practice of studying surface-level information of first one culture and then another without pursuing any aspects of these cultures in depth. For example, the Parent Teacher Organization Committee on the Cultural Arts had brought in three Jewish storytellers and musicians as well as a Native American storyteller and dancer. This committee and the music teacher had arranged for an artist in residence to teach about the various types of music, such as gospel, jazz, and blues, which have African American roots.

One of the school functions of which the administrators were most proud was the annual Multicultural Night. Ms. Greenspan had organized Multicultural Night as a way for the families at Woodlawn to learn about one another's cultures. Booths set up by various families around the Woodlawn gymnasium featured food, clothing, and other artifacts that represented their cultural background. Some of the students and parents also performed traditional dance and music. This year, Multicultural Night had been replaced by a Bread Bazaar. Each of the classes at Woodlawn was responsible for setting up a booth representing a specific country. This booth was to provide some sort of information about the country as well as a type of bread or other dietary staple for people to taste as they viewed the exhibits. Throughout the day, each class was scheduled to dance a traditional dance from the country that they were representing at the Bread Bazaar.

Ms. Greenspan explained that functions such as the Bread Bazaar and Multicultural Night were ways for people at Woodlawn to come together and interact with one another as well as ways to open doors for parents who may not feel comfortable in the school environment. Although Woodlawn had a very active Parent Teacher Organization comprised of white, mainly middle-class, families, there was also a group of parents who weren't involved in the school. The Woodlawn staff invested a great deal of time and effort in what was referred to as "community building."

For example, the school applied for and received a $1,000 federal grant last year to reach out to nonwhite low-income families. The Parent Cooperative, the program created to fulfill this goal, was headed by Ms. Greenspan. It consisted of two African American, two Hmong, two Laotian, and two Cambodian parents who were given a small stipend to act as liaisons between the school and their respective cultural communities. The role of the Parent Cooperative was to keep families of color abreast of the activities at Woodlawn so that they could feel that they had a stake in the school. The Parent Cooperative was featured at the April Parent Teacher Organization meeting, which was held in the new Archer Avenue Head Start building. Holding the PTO meeting in the Archer Avenue neighborhood was another strategy for community building. Because many of the families did not own a car, the staff at Woodlawn often traveled to the parents. Transportation to other school events was provided by the school. There was a real commitment on the part of the staff to make connections with all of the parents at Woodlawn.

Even with all of these programs in place, Ms. Greenspan felt that many of the parents at Woodlawn were not involved in school activities:

> Well, it isn't because of this school; it's just schools in general. Many of them are minority parents who already feel that they are being discriminated against or oppressed. And school is one more system that fosters that idea. As I said, some don't speak English. Some had poor experiences in school or not a lot of educational experiences themselves so they don't feel comfortable here.

The faculty and staff at Woodlawn did attempt to form better relations among themselves and families of color through activities such as those mentioned above. Underlying all of the talk and action however, is the assumption that the students and families who are not members of the dominant culture are "other." In order to gain legitimate membership in the school community, members of nondominant cultures have to appropriate the ways of thinking, speaking, and acting that are associated with the children and parents who are white and middle class. It is not surprising that students and families of color would feel uncomfortable and discriminated against as Ms. Greenspan suggests, in an environment that does not acknowledge or validate their cultural norms.

The Genre of Woodlawn Elementary

The discourse of normalization which pervades the genre at Woodlawn Elementary grows out of the history of the norms that surrounded Woodlawn when it was a predominately white middle-to-upper-middle-class neighborhood school. Woodlawn faculty and staff expect that all children and their families will adapt to the school norms rather than seeing themselves as having to respond to the changing needs of a more heterogeneous population.

Children of color from Archer Avenue were seen as "others" in relation to those children from the Wonago neighborhood who were white and middle class. Further complicating this construction, the African American children from Archer Avenue were "othered" differently from their peers of Asian decent. A hierarchy of deficits existed between these two groups of children. African American children were seen as being the most deficient because their behavior varied most obviously from the norm. Asian children were conceived of as being "foreign," yet the "appropriate behaviors" that they exhibited constructed them as being closer to the norm than their African American peers. Chapter 5 examines these constructions more fully within the context of Ms. Nicholi's kindergarten classroom.

CHAPTER FIVE

Ms. Nicholi's Kindergarten

Ms. Nicholi makes a left turn in her red Chevy Cavalier as she comments to me, "This is where it starts. The Archer Avenue neighborhood starts right here." She continues to drive slowly past the large brick apartment complexes that are built so close together they look as if they are in a huddle trying to stave off the blustery winter wind. Some of the shutters are missing or hanging askew, and the paint is faded on the trim around many of the windows and doors. A few rusted-out cars rest in the driveways that lead up to the apartment buildings. It is so cold this afternoon that the neighborhood looks almost deserted except for three young African American men who are standing on the street corner laughing and talking with one another. Snowflakes drift onto the windshield as Ms. Nicholi remarks, "Most of the children in my class live in two-bedroom apartments, like Dia—she lives with her parents and eight siblings." As we near an intersection, Ms. Nicholi stops the car and points out the community center where she had worked during the summer. She then turns the car around so that we can drive past the new Head Start building before we get onto the highway and head back to Woodlawn Elementary School. As we leave the Archer Avenue neighborhood behind, Ms. Nicholi comments, " I think this will help you to understand what you see when you begin your observations in my classroom."

Anne Nicholi is a twenty-eight-year-old, second-generation Italian American woman. She grew up in Grandville, Illinois, which she describes as a "white middle-class suburb of Chicago." She attended Catholic school for twelve years in Grandville before moving to Mayfield to attend Midwestern University.

Miss Nicholi did not set out to be an early childhood teacher. Originally, she graduated from Midwestern University with a degree in political science with hopes of becoming a juvenile lawyer. After working as an intern in the Legal Defense Program as an undergraduate, Ms. Nicholi changed her mind.

As an intern, it had been Ms. Nicholi's job to take statements from juveniles who had been involved in criminal misdemeanor cases. It was during this internship that Ms. Nicholi began to think about teaching as a career. In her words:

> I was seeing all these kids come through who basically were pretty messed up. And I just felt like you know . . . if I could have only talked to them earlier, I could have helped them. If they had someone in their life who had showed them, like their mom or who cared about them. They were just so hard and really lost. Really sad kids. Messed up. You would want to say, "What are you doing? You're messing up your whole life!"

Ms. Nicholi began to wonder whether the best way for her to reach young people before they, like the juvenile offenders with whom she worked, could get into trouble was to become an early childhood teacher. It was at this point that she made the decision to apply to the teacher education program at Midwestern and was accepted as a Child and Family Studies student in the Early Education Program. At the same moment that she was accepted into the program, she made a commitment to herself that she would focus her efforts on children "at risk." Ms. Nicholi explained:

> I wanted to teach kids at risk. I wanted to make a difference in kids' lives. I wanted a job that was important. That you go to and you're doing good. You're helping. . . . Even if it's in a small way you're doing something. I wanted to be needed and I wanted to make a difference. And I wanted to feel good about what I did.

Ms. Nicholi graduated from the EEP in December and was hired as an educational assistant in the spring at Woodlawn Elementary. She floated among four high-needs elementary classes and worked with classroom teachers to provide additional educational instruction to small groups of children. In her words, "There were a lot of high-needs kids in the rooms, and the teachers weren't able to meet the needs of all of their kids for reading groups and stuff. I was specifically hired to work with the kids."

The following fall, Ms. Nicholi was hired as one of four full-time kindergarten magnet teachers at Woodlawn. In light of Ms. Nicholi's desire to work with "at risk" students, a kindergarten magnet classroom at Woodlawn was exactly the type of program in which she desired to teach. Like the other faculty and staff members at Woodlawn, she made a distinction between the children in her class from Archer Avenue and those who were not. On our very first meeting, she suggested that to help me understand what I would be observing we visit the Archer Avenue neighborhood so that I could get a sense of the home situations of the children in her classroom.

The Kindergarten Classroom

There are eighteen kindergartners in Ms. Nicholi's class that she describes as being "some of the neediest kids you've ever seen." Demographically the class consists of six African American children (three boys and two girls), five Southeast Asian children (four girls and one boy), one East Asian boy, and six white children (three girls and three boys). The five Southeast Asian children speak primarily Hmong and are enrolled in the English as a Second Language program. Twelve of the eighteen kindergartners reside in the Archer Avenue neighborhood.

The physical appearance of Ms. Nicholi's kindergarten classroom can best be described as large, colorful, and inviting. Sunlight streams through the windows that overlook the grass and trees of the schoolyard. Elaborate bulletin board displays are changed often to feature the artwork of Ms. Nicholi and the children. A dramatic play area that regularly undergoes many exciting transformations is organized to parallel the thematic units that Ms. Nicholi presents to the children. It has become, at various times, a restaurant, bus station, post office, flower shop, and a pond. The props provided for the imaginative play of the kindergartners are quite elaborate. For example, a huge tub of plastic flowers, ribbons, and different types of vases as well as a cash register and play money are made available to the children when the dramatic play area becomes a flower shop.

The classroom is organized with the interests of the children in mind. A block area, book corner, water table, invention center, computer, and two easels are positioned around the room. Five child-sized tables with chairs are grouped on one side of the room. A large piece of gray carpet is placed on the other side of the room. Large-group discussions and whole-group activities take place here.

The Five Little Carrots

The children are sitting in a semi-circle on the large square of gray carpet in the middle of the room. Ms. Nicholi is leading the kindergartners in a chant of "The Five Little Carrots," which is written on chart paper and hanging on the easel in the front of the room. After they finish the chant, Ms. Nicholi passes out the books in which they have been copying and illustrating the chant. She reminds them not to open their books until she is through passing them out to everyone. Using her book as a guide, she opens the cover and directs the children to do so as well. "I want you to open to page one, two, three, four, five, six," counts Ms. Nicholi as she slowly turns each page. The children follow her lead. Ms. Nicholi picks up the pencils that are in front of her and passes one to each child as she says, "When I give you your pencil, put it right on the spot in the book where you are going to start writing."

The children stretch out on their stomachs as they position themselves to write. Most of them have their pencils pointed to the spot where they are going to begin to print. Ms. Nicholi walks around to each child, repositioning the pencils of those who don't seem to have it quite right. Ms. Nicholi then walks back up to the front of the room, points to the sixth line in the chant, and reads, "Do you like to eat carrots?" She then specifies, "This is the sentence that we are working on."

The children are asked to sound out the letters in each word. Ms. Nicholi exaggerates the movement of her mouth as she sounds out the first word which begins with the letter "d." She asks the children to sound it out. A few of the children make the "d" sound, but many other sounds are voiced as well. "Did you hear that?" asks Ms. Nicholi. She writes the letter "d" on the dry erase board and directs the children to copy the letter down on their papers. "What's the letter we're writing?," she asks. Some children shout out, "d." Ms. Nicholi nods her head indicating that "d" is correct. Referring to herself in the third person, she says, "Look how Ms. Nicholi made her "d." Is it sloppy?" The children answer, "No." Ms. Nicholi reminds the children, "Do your best work."

If you just made a "d," put your hands on your head," directs Ms. Nicholi. Letter by letter they spell out the word "you." If you wrote Y-O-U, make a U in the air with your hands so that I know you're done," directs Ms. Nicholi. "I'm done!" shouts Wayne as he throws his arms into the air.

Wayne's "I'm done" has caught on. As the children write the next letter several of them shout "I'm done!" Ms. Nicholi, asks if anyone wants to write the sentence, "I will not shout when I'm done writing a letter." Maureen says, "Ooh, that's 10 words!" No one shouts after they finish writing the next letter although there are some very softly whispered "I'm dones."

A Teacher Directed Program

The above vignette illustrates that Ms. Nicholi's classroom is both teacher directed and skill oriented. Although children are provided with the opportunity to play and make some choices about their activities during planning centers, the focus of this kindergarten classroom is one of mastering basic skills. "Basic skills" in this context refers to the reading, writing, and mathematics competencies that are taught to children through the use of worksheets or projects that promote learning through drill and practice. Ms. Nicholi does not specifically refer to her curriculum as one that promotes basic skills, but she does characterize herself as a "traditional teacher." From her perspective, a traditional view of teaching includes teaching number and letter recognition as well as letter sounds. For example, she states:

> Being a teacher and the traditional view is a big part, especially of the kindergarten years. I'm here to teach them things. I want them to learn. I want them to learn what they need to progress in school. I want them to learn their numbers, their letters, and their sounds. I want them to learn work habits, to take pride in their work. I want them to learn how to share, how to be friends, how to be independent. The things that are important to function in society, to move on; the rules to live by.

Reading and writing skills are emphasized most heavily, and as the vignette illustrates, it is typical for children to be drilled on letter recognition, letter sounds, the use of upper and lower case letters, and the use of correct punctuation. The detailed directions that Ms. Nicholi gives to the children as they work on this assignment are typical of the amount of the direction that children receive on every activity in which they are asked to engage.

The following is an example of the typical daily schedule that varies little from day to day:

journaling

calendar

planning centers

project

music

recess

lunch

rest and relaxation

math

project

recess

home

The kindergartners arrive at school between 8:00 A.M. and 8:20 A.M. Since twelve of the eighteen children in Ms. Nicholi's kindergarten class are eligible for the free breakfast program, they arrive at school earlier than the other children. As children finish breakfast, they head down to the kindergarten room.

Each day, Ms. Nicholi writes a morning message on the board. The morning message reads something like this:

Good Morning,
    Today is Monday. We have music. Do you think it will rain?
    Love,
    Ms. N

Children are encouraged to copy the morning message in their journal if they cannot think of anything to write or draw on their own, and this is what most children choose to do. Ms. Nicholi works individually with each child as she takes dictation, corrects words that are misspelled, and reforms letters that the children have printed. Children receive stickers or stamps for completing their journal entries and are then directed to choose a book from Ms. Nicholi's collection, sit quietly on the carpet, and read.

After journaling, the kindergartners come together on the carpet for a short group time. Ms. Nicholi changes the date on the calendar, takes attendance, and counts the number of children who are going to receive either hot or cold lunch. She then explains the activities that are going to be available to the kindergartners during planning center time, when children can choose to work or play at a variety of locations around the room. Planning centers include the dramatic play area, the building block center, the art center, a science center, a computer center, and a listening center where children can listen to a book on tape.

A language arts project, such as the one featured in the "Five Little Carrots" vignette, follows planning centers. Typically, Ms. Nicholi reads the kindergartners a book or introduces them to a new poem or chant. The reading is then tied to a project that is usually a worksheet or a comparable activity created by Ms. Nicholi. A similar type of project is also presented to the kindergartners in the afternoon.

Ms. Nicholi believes that the kindergartners need to run and play outdoors, not simply for exercise but also as a means to release energy not expended at home. Her concern is that such unreleased energy might impact the classroom negatively. She takes the children outside for recess whenever weather permits. In addition to the recess that the children have after lunch, two other fifteen-minute recesses are scheduled during the day, one in the morning and the other in the afternoon.

Ms. Nicholi explains that this type of regimented curriculum was not what she had imagined at the beginning of the school year. She says:

> How you see the room when you walk in now, the structure of the room—not the physical environment but the order of things and how class is conducted—has changed. Because at the beginning of the year, I didn't do a plan on the board. I had manipulatives on the tables; I didn't have journal writing, and I didn't have them sit in assigned seats. I had them sit wherever they wanted; I didn't assign groups at tables. I gave them choices but they weren't ready for that and it led to a lot of social problems. The problems were about sharing or not wanting to be next to a certain person or just competing for a special toy.

Ms. Nicholi's initial desire was to gear the classroom arrangement toward the developmental needs and interests of the kindergartners, but the difficulty the children exhibited over making choices led Ms. Nicholi to the conclusion that the children were "not developmentally ready" for the opportunities that she had provided for them. In her words:

> They wanted to know what they needed to do. It was too open. They could go to any of the tables, and they could play with any of four things. It was too many choices. I think the kids in my classroom really rely on structure and routine. They didn't know if the blocks would be out tomorrow; they didn't know if they would get a turn.

Ms. Nicholi draws on the discourse of child-centeredness as she defines the developmental needs of the kindergartners and plans her classroom design. She locates the reason for adhering to such a strict schedule within the individual children and families with whom she works. She describes the family lives of her children as being chaotic and uncontrolled, so she works to provide the stability and predictability in the classroom that she feels they are not receiving at home. She says:

> They need the predictability of it. That's really comfortable knowing when it's going to happen. . . . Because they don't have control over so many other things. I mean I think a lot of it is, "Okay, it's time to go." They don't know when things are happening. They don't know when someone is going to come in exploding. When someone walks in the door, they can be in a good mood, or they can be in a rotten mood. When Mom's boyfriend comes over, he can be silly, happy, playful, or he can be drunk and angry. They don't know what's coming on for schedules of things. They don't know if this weekend they're going to Chicago, or they don't know if they're going to play with their cousins. I mean even the kids that don't have homes like that. It's just really important to know what's coming next.

The above passage is replete with references to the social issues that affect some of the Archer Avenue families. The reference to Chicago and "playing with cousins" refers to the two children in Ms. Nicholi's classroom and a number of children at Woodlawn in general who have experienced homelessness. A typical practice that is followed by the Archer Avenue families who are in transition is to move around Mayfield, Chicago, and another large city as they search for housing. Oftentimes, these moves are to join other family members such as the cousins to whom Ms. Nicholi refers.

Certainly, pedagogy which is basic skills oriented and teacher directed can lead to positive learning experiences for children (for example, see Delpit, 1995; Ladson-Billings, 1994). However, what is problematic here is that Ms. Nicholi has lowered her expectations for the kindergartners in her class. What is being promoted in the kindergarten is an emphasis on basic skills and work habits which lead to conforming behaviors, not the development of higher-order thinking skills such as creative problem-solving or critical thinking. From Ms. Nicholi's perspective, the children in her kindergarten don't have the resources behaviorally or intellectually to pursue activities which promote these higher-order thinking skills. In order to impose "appropriate behaviors," Ms. Nicholi draws extensively on the discourse of behaviorism as she carries out her basic skills oriented, teacher directed pedagogy.

"The Five Little Carrots" reveals that Ms. Nicholi expects the children not only to follow her directions but also to imitate precisely the way that she is shaping her letters with her hand as she writes and with her mouth as she sounds out each letter. All children start with their pencils on the same spot on the paper and work on the same letter that is being modeled for them to print.

Children were asked to duplicate the products made by Ms. Nicholi in every activity that I observed except one. When children were asked to complete an activity, Ms. Nicholi gave explicit directions, which she repeated an average of three times. The children were then asked to repeat the exact sequence of steps in which they were to complete their work. Conformity and work habits were praised as Ms. Nicholi circulated around the room complimenting individual children for things such as "remembering to use pencil first, then pen" or "following directions nicely."

Through a discourse of behaviorism, Ms. Nicholi shapes the behaviors of the children in her class as she sets up a relationship with them in which she holds the authority and the knowledge in the classroom. As she explains, "I think it's important in kindergarten that they know that I'm the teacher, and they have to do things because I'm the teacher." According to a behaviorist perspective, if children are engaged in activities and lessons that promote drill and repetition, appropriate behaviors and responses will eventually become ingrained in their minds.

Ms. Nicholi attempted to elicit and control "appropriate behaviors" from the kindergartners with the use of rewards. The definition of "appropriate behaviors" that circulated around Ms. Nicholi's kindergarten classroom paralleled those behaviors that were sanctioned by the other faculty and staff members at Woodlawn. The "appropriate behaviors" included the concepts of "polite," "well behaved," and "able to control one's own actions." The noise level was low. The children followed directions, paid attention, and walked in a line. Most of the children were, indeed, polite and well behaved; however, the children who couldn't always maintain such behaviors were publicly and consistently constructed as deficient through the withholding of snacks and rewards.

Two systems of rewards were used in the classroom to reinforce the desired behaviors. Short-term rewards for behavior usually consisted of snacks such as crackers, cookies, or fruit. Long-term rewards consisted of badges that were awarded to children in a "badge ceremony" at the end of each day.

Morning snack, a short-term reward, was frequently used as an incentive for children to sit quietly or pay attention during the explanation of the morning project. Consider the following passage from my field notes:

> Ms. Nicholi has just finished reading. Some children are complaining that they can't see. Ms. Nicholi goes back through each of the pages and recaps the story. She stops to talk about mobile homes. Christopher proceeds to tell the class that his grandmother lives in a mobile home. The children discuss the different types of homes that are represented in the book. Ms. Nicholi says, "It's time to do the project. When I see you being a good listener, I will give you a cookie. What's a good listener?" As Ms. Nicholi lists the qualities of a good listener, some of the children say them with her. The children sit up a little straighter and look a little more attentive . . . (ten minutes later). . . Ms. Nicholi finishes explaining the project, and the children are directed to move from the carpet to their tables. Tim walks over to Ms. Nicholi and asks, "Can you give us some snack now?" Ms. Nicholi looks directly at Tim and responds, "When I see you working." She then addresses the class and says, "This is your best work. Your best drawings."

Shortly after Tim's request, Ms. Nicholi did pass out the cookies. She went by each seat and checked to see that the children were working before handing them a cookie. Snacks were rewarded in this manner for other behaviors such as "holding bodies in the right way," "sitting in a listening position," "cleaning up," "getting into outdoor winter clothing quickly," and "raising hands to talk."

Through edible rewards, Ms. Nicholi provides the external stimuli that evoke the behaviors that she deems appropriate for children. The rewards are not immediate but rather are contingent upon the behaviors exhibited by a child over a short period of time. As Ms. Nicholi says, "I don't put snack up on the schedule because it might have to be changed. I don't want them to expect it at a certain time . . . I use that as a carrot." While snacks provide short-term motivation for appropriate behaviors, long-term motivation is supported by the badge ceremony that takes place at the end of each day. The badges, made of construction paper and decorated with glitter, are awarded to the three children she judges to be "best listener," "best hall walker," and "best friend" in the kindergarten on that day.

Quite an elaborate ritual surrounds the awarding of the badges. Ms. Nicholi directs the kindergartners to produce a drum roll by clapping their hands on their knees. She then awards the badges one by one. As the three children's names are called out, each child comes to the front of the room and stands next to Ms. Nicholi. She explains why the child has won the award and then tapes it to their clothing. The award winners are then the first to be dismissed from the carpet so that they can be the first in line to go home.

Presenting children with rewards for appropriate behaviors was a common practice, so too was the use of punishments for inappropriate behaviors. Punishments included writing sentences, being given a time out, missing the first five to ten minutes of recess or planning center time or, in extreme cases, being physically removed from the classroom. The punishment that Ms. Nicholi used most frequently was assigning the kindergartners sentences to write pertaining to their misbehavior. For example, in the earlier vignette, when the children began shouting out "I'm done!," Ms. Nicholi simply asked if they wanted to write "I will not shout when I am done writing a letter." This was a fairly effective technique. Children did not like to take the time to sit and write sentences, and often the "inappropriate behavior" immediately subsided. Ms. Nicholi commented that she had learned through the course of the year that she needed to have clear consequences in place for things such as speaking out of turn on the rug:

> I guess I just learned that if you let one kid get away with something like speaking out of turn on the rug . . . things would just get out of control. Things just escalate. There needs to be a consequence for that kind of behavior, otherwise everyone would do it and it would just be chaos. If you don't make it a punishment or if you don't make a big deal out of something that only one or two kids do, they all start doing it.

In order to keep the classroom running smoothly, Ms. Nicholi felt that she had to punish those children who were exhibiting "inappropriate behaviors." Punishment, in her mind, was the way to forestall things before they get beyond her control. The idea of having a controlled classroom in this context meant that all of the children were exhibiting those behaviors considered appropriate within the predominant discourse of normalization at Woodlawn.

Together, variants of the discourse of child-centeredness and the discourse of behaviorism created a discourse of normalization in Ms. Nicholi's kindergarten that generated the conformity and homogeneity that she valued and rewarded. Ms. Nicholi worked toward the creation of the "ideal kindergartner" who lives within the discourse of normalization. From her perspective, the prototypical kindergartner is well versed in basic skills, is between 60 and 71 months old, and is socialized to the white middle-class ways of speaking and acting that are sanctioned by the faculty and staff at Woodlawn School.

Searching for the Ideal Kindergartner

Ms. Nicholi works hard to shape each of the children in her care into the ideal kindergartner. She relies on her understanding of development and diversity to shape the way that she perceives individual children and defines the types of curriculum and instruction that she presents to them. Yet, she finds that none of the children in this kindergarten fits the vision towards which she is working. Some children are too young and immature; others are too needy and emotional, and others she just can't understand.

Among the children she regarded as too young and immature were four kindergartners to whom she referred as the "young fives." The birthdays of these children fell in the summer months of June, July, and August. Ms. Nicholi expressed her reservations about the maturity level of the young fives, including that of Tim who was considered a role model at Woodlawn.

Tim, a white male, utilized an extensive vocabulary and was extremely knowledgeable about mammal and marine life. For example, as the class was making an alphabet animal book, they were having difficulty thinking of the name of an animal that began with the letter "I." Tim suggested that they use ibex and offered to draw the picture. An instance of Tim's use of vocabulary occurred one morning on the playground. As the kindergarten class was standing in line waiting to walk back into the building, two older boys had a head-on collision and fell down in the snow. Witnessing the accident, Ms. Nicholi remarked, "Oooh, those two boys collided." Tim, who was standing near the head of the line, asked Ms. Nicholi to define the word "collide." She explained that the word meant that two things had run into each other. Later that morning, Tim appropriately used the word "collide" in the context of a large-group discussion.

Observing this incident, I commented on his use of the word and his vocabulary in general to Ms. Nicholi. Although she agreed that cognitively he was ahead of many of his peers, she pointed to the colorful cardboard birthday balloons hanging above the alphabet stapled to the wall and commented:

> Intellectually he knows a lot, but his birthday is August 22nd. He's a young five. His fine motor skills and social skills are so behind. I just don't know what to do with him.

There were other instances in which Ms. Nicholi pointed out Tim's shortcomings, such as his coloring, which she referred to as "scribbles." By February, Ms. Nicholi had spoken with Tim's parents about the possibility of retention. Developmentally, she just didn't believe that he was ready for first grade. In her words:

> You know he's going to have to go to first grade next year, and it's not like this. It's very structured, and he's not ready for it. He is smart, but he's an August 22nd birthday. He is just so behind socially and emotionally. He just acts like a toddler.

Ms. Nicholi went on to say that if Tim repeated kindergarten he "would have more friends, and his fine motor skills would have time to develop." Ms. Nicholi perceived Tim as being cognitively able, but because her understanding of development was so tied to notions of age, the fact that his birthday fell at the end of August automatically negated his intellectual abilities. Instead, Ms. Nicholi focused her attention on what she perceived to be the areas in which Tim was lacking in development.

Ms. Nicholi was introduced to this notion of development through the course work and activities that she encountered as a prospective teacher in the EEP. Recall the midterm in the course, "Social and Emotional Development in Young Children," which specifically assessed the ability of prospective teachers to diagnose the various levels of development that a fictional child was experiencing.

Diagnosing the development of each child is a practice that is carried out schoolwide at Woodlawn. At the beginning of the academic year, each student is assessed in order to identify her/his levels of development across a variety of areas. The idea is that children will then be presented with curriculum and instruction according to their individual developmental needs.

Ms. Nicholi appropriates this practice of diagnosing development as she makes decisions about Tim's school career and the careers of the other children in her classroom. Drawing on the meaning of development as it is conceptualized within the discourse of child-centeredness, Ms. Nicholi believes that the problem of the "young fives," such as Tim, is immaturity. She believes that by retaining Tim she can provide him with the "gift of time" (Graue, 1993, p. 2), which will allow him to grow and develop into the model child that lives within the discourse of normalization.

76   The Social Fashioning of Teacher Identities

Shawn, Wayne, and the majority of the poor African American children, like the young fives, don't meet the standards that are set for the ideal kindergartner either. However, Ms. Nicholi does not perceive Shawn and Wayne as needing more time to mature, as she assumes to be the case with Tim. Rather, she perceives their emotional and behavioral problems as stemming from their family situations and as residing within the children themselves. The following vignette illustrates an interaction between Ms. Nicholi and Shawn and highlights the anger and frustration that were prevalent among African American males in this classroom.

Whiting It Out

The children are seated on the carpet in a semicircle. Ms. Nicholi is introducing the morning project. There is a white legal-sized piece of paper with the outline of a body Xeroxed in the middle. The words "I have a band-aid on my _____" are written across the top of the paper. Ms. Nicholi asks the children to count the number of words in the sentence. The children count as Ms. Nicholi points to each word, "One, two, three, four, five, six, and a space!" Ms. Nicholi asks the children to help her read the words. A few children attempt to sound out the letters as she points to each word.

After they have finished reading the sentence, Ms. Nicholi asks if there is a volunteer who would like to come up and place the band-aid on the drawing of the person. Several hands shoot up into the air. Ms. Nicholi calls on Shawn, who smiles and walks to the front of the class. He stands next to Ms. Nicholi, who hands him a band-aid.

Ms. Nicholi explains to the children that they can place the band-aid anywhere that they choose on the outline of the body. Ms. Nicholi turns to Shawn, "So Shawn, where are you going to put the band-aid?" Shawn answers that he is going to put it on the forehead. "Forehead," says Ms. Nicholi slowly and deliberately. "How do we spell forehead?" She sounds out each letter with the kindergartners as she writes the word "forehead" very neatly on the line that she has provided on the paper.

Ms. Nicholi turns to Shawn and asks him to open the wrapper of the band-aid. She looks at the group of kindergartners and asks, "Where are we going to put the wrappers after we open them?" The children answer, "In the garbage." As Shawn begins to tear the paper wrapper off of the band-aid, Ms. Nicholi asks, "Do you know how to open a band-aid, honey?" Nodding his head to indicate "yes," Shawn continues opening the wrapper. Ms. Nicholi says, "Some children don't," as she proceeds to take the band-aid out of Shawn's hands. Very slowly she explains the right way to open band-aids, "You try not to touch that white part. Do you know why?" Without waiting for an answer she remarks, "Because if you touch it, you put germs on it. You want to keep it clean. See how I'm holding the sides."

After she opens the band-aid, Ms. Nicholi hands it back to Shawn and directs him to put it onto the forehead of the person. Ms. Nicholi compliments Shawn on his work and then sends him back to his spot on the carpet.

"So," says Ms. Nicholi, addressing the children, "the first thing you do is place the band-aid on the picture. Oops, the first thing we are going to do before we do anything else is write our. . . .?" The children respond, "Name."

"Right," says Ms. Nicholi, smiling as she picks up her pencil and writes her name on the paper. Ms. Nicholi repeats, "The first thing we do is write our name. The second thing you do is decide where you want to put the band-aid. The third thing you do is you have to make it look like you. How many eyes do I have?"

The children shout, "Two!" "What color are my eyes?," asks Ms. Nicholi. The children yell out a variety of colors. Ms. Nicholi responds that they are brown. She then picks out her brown crayon, and colors the eyes of the picture brown.

Ms. Nicholi then asks, "What is in the middle of my face?"

Some children shout out, "Nose!"

Wayne laughs and shouts, "A big, big nose!"

Ms. Nicholi laughs and asks, "Do I have a big nose?"

Jerry replies, "Bigger than ours."

Ms. Nicholi continues this question-and-answer process for her hair, blouse, skirt, and shoes. She colors each article of clothing the same color as the clothing that she is wearing.

Ms. Nicholi asks as she colors, "Am I coloring in the lines?"

The children answer, "Yes."

Ms. Nicholi explains that she wants them to color in the lines just as she is doing. "I want you to take your time and do your best job. Your best coloring and your best writing."

After Ms. Nicholi explains the directions one more time, she passes out one paper to each child and directs them to go back to their seats and get started. Ms. Nicholi circulates around the room as the children work. She praises children for being neat and helps children to spell words and to shape their letters.

Shawn is sitting at his seat with his head in his hands, "I can't do this!," he shouts as he throws his paper on the floor. He then stands up, picks up his chair, and throws it on the floor as he yells, "I hate this stupid old school!"

Ms. Nicholi, who is helping Chloe with her printing, says to Shawn, "Where am I? I'm here to help you. Raise your hand." Ms. Nicholi continues working with Chloe as Shawn stamps over to the door and shouts, "I'm going to slam the door now!" "Not unless you want to take a time out in TLC," responds Ms. Nicholi calmly.

Ms. Nicholi walks across the room and stands in front of Shawn, "I keep on messin' up!" he shouts as tears begin to stream down his face.

Together they walk back over to the table. Ms. Nicholi picks the paper up off of the floor and asks, "What's wrong, why don't you like it?"

"That!" he answers, pointing to the uneven letters that he has printed on the page.

Ms. Nicholi asks, *"Do you know why? It's because you used pen instead of pencil. Now you can't erase it. Let Ms. N. go get her white paint."*

Ms. Nicholi walks over to her desk and takes out a bottle of white-out. She walks back over to Shawn's table and paints over his "mistakes." Ms. Nicholi reminds him, "Let the paint dry before you try to write the letters over again."

Imposing Identities

In Ms. Nicholi's classroom frustration and anger went hand in hand. Outbursts such as the one exhibited by Shawn as he attempted to print his letters were a frequent occurrence. Shawn could print; he was an inventive speller, and he understood the concept of a sentence. Yet, when the printing was not perfectly positioned on the lined paper or when he used invented spelling in his writing, Ms. Nicholi would invalidate his work by whiting it out and asking him to rewrite the work that he had just completed. On the day of this particular band-aid lesson, Ms. Nicholi returned to Shawn's desk after approximately eight minutes to check his work again. Shawn had rewritten the sentence in letters that dangled off the lines on the paper. Ms. Nicholi read the sentence, turned to Shawn and said to him in front of everyone, "This is not your best work. Erase these two words and write them correctly, or you will have to do the whole page over. It's your choice." As she walked away from Shawn's desk, he began to cry and kick the legs of the table at which he was sitting. Ms. Nicholi then turned to Shawn and repeated, "Make your choice."

The outbursts exhibited by Shawn and Wayne ranged from shouting, to throwing papers and pencils on the floor, to the less frequent kicking and knocking over of furniture. Over the course of my visits to Woodlawn, Wayne and Shawn, six-year-old African American males, had both been suspended for their angry outbursts, Wayne three times and Shawn twice. One afternoon, Ms. Nicholi showed me a bruise on the underside of her arm where Shawn had grabbed her in a fit of anger and refused to let go. She resorted to carrying him to the TLC room, and the principal subsequently suspended him. Ms. Nicholi discussed the ways in which the behaviors of the children in her class differed from those exhibited by kindergartners in general:

> All kindergartners are needy, but there are a lot of kids that have real special needs. Just the clinging. They're very clingy. And they're very angry about things beyond the task. You see that immediately. They get so angry, and it has nothing to do with what you're asking them to do. Nothing to do with the project that they're working on. I don't feel like I have a lot of strategies on how to help kids overcome all that anger and to feel successful and to deal with their frustration and to help them with their own problems. I mean classroom management, behavior management, and those kinds of issues.

Within a discourse of child-centeredness, Ms. Nicholi locates the anger and frustration within each individual child. She sees her responsibility in this situation as building up her repertoire of behavior management techniques in order to help children deal more effectively with their own behaviors.

One possible explanation for the frustration and anger exhibited by the children of color in this class is the lack of acknowledgment of their talents and personal knowledge. In "Whiting It Out" Shawn isn't given the opportunity to show the class that he can open the wrapper on a band-aid properly nor is it acknowledged that he can print and spell. Ms. Nicholi disempowers the children by denying that they bring their own expert knowledge into the school (Delpit, 1995, p. 33).

The variant of the discourse of behaviorism and the variant of the discourse of child-centeredness that Ms. Nicholi draws upon form a discourse of normalization. Through this normalizing discourse, Ms. Nicholi perceives the frustration and anger that some of the males of color in this classroom exhibit as springing from a deficit model. Shawn and Wayne's behaviors are so far outside of the boundaries of what Ms. Nicholi considers appropriate that she no longer feels that their needs can be met in the regular classroom. On the same day that Ms. Nicholi shared with me that she had spoken to Tim's parents about retention, she also disclosed that she had referred Shawn and Wayne for special education services. In her words:

> I also brought Shawn and Wayne up to building team this month. I think they need it. It was hard. I think they are either LD or ED and I think there's been abuse too. It was hard to make a case, but once I did and talked to the team I realized that was not like other classes. The other classes don't have kids like this. Mine is really different.

From the perspective of Ms. Nicholi, the "inappropriate behaviors" exhibited by Shawn and Wayne stem from some abnormality that she can't name. She concludes that, regardless of the source of the behaviors, these children need special help beyond that which can be given in a regular classroom setting.

Within the discourse of normalization, the social identities of Lonnie, Koua, Dia, Sherrie, and Marilyn, the Southeast Asian children, and Xiou, the East Asian child, were constructed much differently from those of the African American children. The five Southeast Asian children, who are Hmong refugees and live in the Archer Avenue area, played together and worked together when they had the chance, and, even though four of the five students were proficient at English, they chose to converse with one another in Hmong. Ms. Nicholi referred to Koua, who was the newest child to the kindergarten, as being "fresh off the boat." Ms. Nicholi perceived this group of Southeast Asian children as immigrants who spoke in a language that, in her words, she "didn't even try to understand." Even though Xiou is not Hmong and interacted more often with non-Asian children, he was still constructed as part of a collective group of Asian students. This was evident in Ms. Nicholi's description of her class as being comprised of "six white students, six African American students, and six Asian students."

The "Asian" children in the kindergarten often seemed to be invisible. Unlike the African American children, the "Asian" children were not reprimanded for "inappropriate behaviors" because the behaviors that they exhibited generally fell within the bounds of what was considered "normal" in the kindergarten classroom. Academically, the children asked for little help from Ms. Nicholi. Although she did help children with their work in a limited manner and rewarded them for their work habits and other "appropriate" behaviors, there was little interaction between the "Asian" students and Ms. Nicholi. The five Southeast Asian children made daily trips to the English as a Second Language Program for instruction, and a Hmong interpreter traveled in and out of the classroom. Due to this external support, it was possible for Ms. Nicholi to assume that she needed to take no further steps to incorporate culturally relevant pedagogy (Ladson-Billings, 1994). She didn't find any behavior problems with this group of children, so she just left them to themselves.

My interpretation is that the children of Asian descent in the kindergarten class were constructed collectively as a "model minority," relative to the group of African American children in Ms. Nicholi's class. In the United States, "Asians" and Asian Americans have come to be constructed as model minorities who have gained success through their hard work and determination. Lee (1996), has written about how the image of the model minority acts as a hegemonic device in three ways. First, within the model minority stereotype, all Asian ethnicities are discussed as if they comprise one monolithic group of "Asians." Second, this aggregation of Asian ethnicities constructs all people of Asian descent as experiencing success while denying the material and social struggles in which many of them are engaged. Third, the model minority stereotype sets up groups of Asian individuals as being "good Americans" in relation to other racial and ethnic groups, a social construction that further perpetuates the status quo.[1]

The model minority stereotype that circulates around Ms. Nicholi's classroom is evident in the way that she refers to all of the children and families who are of Asian descent in her classroom as belonging to a single group. Based on the "appropriate behaviors" that are exhibited by this particular group, Ms. Nicholi constructs these children as "good minorities" in relation to the African American children in the kindergarten. While "model minority" might seem to be a positive label for children of Asian descent, it ultimately works to their disadvantage. Within the model minority stereotype, children of Asian descent may not be receiving the type of educational attention and support that they need. Like the African American children, the children of Asian descent do not see themselves or their ways of knowing represented in Ms. Nicholi's teaching or the curriculum. Furthermore, the model minority stereotype allows Ms. Nicholi to pit the "appropriate behaviors" of the children of Asian descent against the "inappropriate behaviors" exhibited by the African American students and to construct them as stemming from deficiencies in the home or the children, as opposed to looking at behavioral differences within the framework of racial oppression (Lee, 1996).

Ms. Nicholi's construction of the East Asian and Southeast Asian children demonstrates some of the constant tensions within and among the notions of normalization, child-centeredness, behaviorism, and institutional and personal notions of race. On one hand, the Hmong students are praised for their adaptation to the behavioral expectations. Within the discourse of child-centeredness for Ms. Nicholi (and quite possibility the school as well), the students' individual needs are met through the interventions of the ESL teacher and aide. Yet there is an acknowledgment (through Ms. Nicholi's discomfort with the Hmong language and the students' tendency to associate exclusively with one another) of a difference that she perceives as "foreign," i.e, not conforming and therefore "negative." Yet, according to the prevailing discourses of normalization within her classroom and the school, she assumes that it is up to the students to adapt and change.

A Tangle of Discourses

Within the discourse of child-centeredness that was sanctioned in the Department of Child and Family Studies at Midwestern University, Ms. Nicholi would be considered a thoughtful teacher—one who observed the children and made connections among the child's level of development, developmental theory, and the teacher's individual practice. Ms. Nicholi exhibits thoughtfulness in the way that she has observed the children in her class and adjusted her curriculum and instruction based on her observations. Her age-specific understanding of developmental theory as well as her understanding of issues of diversity shape the way that she views children like Tim, Shawn, Wayne, and Koua. Within the discourse of child-centeredness, Ms. Nicholi conceptualizes diversity as a characteristic located within these children. She did not believe that she needed to teach multicultural lessons and activities explicitly. In her words, "I don't feel that I do a lot of things that are multicultural because they are just sort of included in what I do." This quotation is reminiscent of the way that diversity was discussed in the "Family and Community Influences on the Young Child" course in which Ms. Nicholi was enrolled at Midwestern. In this course, prospective teachers were engaged in activities such as the "Family Socioeconomic Problem-Solving Project," in which they were asked to describe how families were affected by membership in the particular racial, ethnic, and socioeconomic groups to which they belonged. From this perspective, diversity was conceived of as an individual characteristic rather than a set of social, cultural, historical, and political conditions.

On two occasions, I observed Ms. Nicholi teach lessons that could be construed as an attempt to teach about diversity. The first occurred when Ms. Nicholi introduced some skin-color crayons to the class during a lesson on band-aids. Just as she had colored her dress blue in the picture that was she was modeling for the children to color, she colored her skin a peach color. She directed the children to find the color that most closely resembled their skin and then to color in their bodies. As Ms. Nicholi was passing out the papers on which they were to color, Christopher, an African American boy, began to sing softly to himself, "a white boy, a black girl, a black boy, a white girl" as he pointed to some of his peers in the class and named their skin color.

In this lesson, Ms. Nicholi highlighted the fact that individual children had different colors of skin. As the children worked with one another to match the crayons to their flesh, they discussed the varying shades. Children such as Christopher could identify themselves and others as "black," "brown," "white," or "yellow," but beyond naming skin colors there was no further discussion of the topic.

The second occasion on which issues of diversity were discussed in the classroom occurred during the time period that the kindergarten was preparing to participate in the schoolwide Bread Bazaar. Each class or a pair of classes was assigned a country. The classes were responsible for decorating booths and for providing a type of bread that was representative of that country. Ms. Nicholi's class and one other were assigned the country of Poland. Ms. Nicholi's class had decorated their part of the booth by cutting out from National Geographic magazines and gluing onto construction paper pictures of people from Poland. Underneath each picture were sentences such as "Polish people like flowers."

Only once did Ms. Nicholi move beyond individual characteristics as she attempted to tie the lives of the kindergartners to the larger social, cultural, historical, and political forces in which they are positioned.

A Sociocultural Discourse

Ms. Nicholi drew upon the sociocultural discourse, one of the two discourses that predominated in the EEP, on one occasion during my observations in the classroom. As Ms. Nicholi discussed her teaching, she explained how she tried to put things into a social context for the children. She recalled the visit of a police officer to the classroom:

> I think I try to put things into a social context. I think I try to take situations out of the classroom and into life. Like when the police officer came. "If you hurt someone," he said, "then you go to jail." I don't know if I come right out and say that but I try to. I say, "You can't hit people because there's a consequence." Or, "you can't take things that aren't yours because it's against the law." I try to make it bigger because a lot of these kids know that. They know that from home; they know that from their community; they know that

from cops and from all those TV shows that they watch. I mean they know that legal system better than I knew it as a kindergartner.

It is interesting that when Ms. Nicholi drew upon the sociocultural discourse as she attempted to make the connection between the life of the child and the social context in which they were positioned, it was embedded within a variant of the discourse of behaviorism. The connection that Ms. Nicholi attempted to make for the children was one that highlighted notions of authority and punishment. At the same time the kindergartners were being taught about the authority vested in Ms. Nicholi, they were also being taught about the authority vested in the law. "If you hit, there's a consequence." "If you hurt someone, you go to jail." Ms. Nicholi linked appropriate school behaviors to behaviors that are typically considered appropriate in society.

The Genre of Ms. Nicholi's Kindergarten

The genre that operates within the kindergarten classroom of Ms. Nicholi is a tangle of discourses. A variant of the discourse of behaviorism and a variant of the discourse of child-centeredness intermingle to produce a discourse of normalization. It is worthwhile to examine why Ms. Nicholi chooses to draw upon these particular discourses as she shapes her identity in relation to the students and families with whom she works.

The variant of the discourse of child-centeredness visible in Ms. Nicholi's classroom can be traced back to the discourse of child-centeredness that predominated within the genre of the EEP at Midwestern University. Notions about development, diversity, and becoming a thoughtful teacher can be detected within the genre that circumscribes Ms. Nicholi's kindergarten classroom. Although influences of the discourse of child-centeredness are readily apparent in her speech and actions, there is barely a trace of the critical sociocultural discourse that she also encountered at Midwestern.

The reason that Ms. Nicholi continues to appropriate the discourse of child-centeredness to which she was introduced at Midwestern may be that a localized version of that discourse circumscribes Woodlawn Elementary. Ms. Nicholi retains the discourse of child-centeredness because it is supported by those with whom she works. In her attempt to fit into the school culture and to communicate in meaningful ways with her new colleagues, she draws on the discourse of child-centeredness already in place there.

Ms. Nicholi's ready appropriation of the discourse that surrounds Woodlawn Elementary may be partially attributable to her desire to fit into the school. However, I believe the discourse of normalization is consistent with her personal philosophy of teaching. Ms. Nicholi's desire to teach young children stems from her experiences with juvenile offenders as a law intern. She wants to work with young children whom she considers to be "at risk" because she does not want them to end up like the juvenile offenders with whom she had previously worked. Ms. Nicholi's vision of what it means to be a kindergarten teacher mirrors those values that are advocated at Woodlawn. She emphasizes appropriate behaviors and following the rules in school and society.

Ms. Nicholi's position in society as a white middle-class woman may also be one of the reasons that the discourse of normalization is comfortable for her. As a member of the dominant culture, she receives all of the benefits that come with membership in this particular group. Ms. Nicholi sees no need to challenge the discourse of normalization because it resonates with the privilege that she enjoys in her own personal life.

PART II

The Discursive Fashioning of Ms. Gonzales

CHAPTER SIX

Charting the Genre of Multicultural Education

Multicultural education in the United States grew out of the struggles against racial oppression that took place during the Civil Rights Movement of the 1960s and 1970s (Banks, 1995; Sleeter & Grant, 1987). The Civil Rights Movement challenged educational institutions to make education equitable for all children by changing the content and processes within schools (Sleeter & Grant, 1987). Early proponents of multicultural education focused their attention on issues of race, but the field soon expanded to address issues of gender, class, religious diversity, sexual orientation, and physical ability. While proponents agree that multicultural education is an effort to make schooling more equitable for all children, there is a lack of consensus about the actual definition of the term (Sleeter & Grant, 1987; Sleeter, 1991).[1] Multicultural education has been, and continues to be, a site of contention.

Although multicultural education is a relatively young field, the work of scholars such as W. E. B. DuBois and George Washington Williams laid the foundation almost a century ago (Banks, 1995). Such movements as the Intercultural Education Movement that took place after World War II also helped to shape and form multicultural education as we know it today (Banks, 1995; Olneck, 1990). The following paragraphs briefly trace the discourses that led to the inception of multicultural education and continue to shape the field.

Discourses of Race Consciousness and Race Pride

If there is no struggle, there is no progress. Those who profess to favor freedom and yet deprecate agitation are people who want crops without plowing the ground. They want rain without thunder and lightning. That struggle might be a moral one; it might be a physical one; it might be both moral and physical, but it must be a struggle. Power concedes nothing without a demand. It never did and never will. People might not get all that they work for in this world, but they must certainly work for all they get. (Frederick Douglass, 1857)

There is evidence that as early as 1640 Negro children attended schools in Massachusetts and Virginia alongside their white counterparts (Banks, 1995; Brooks, 1990; White, 1973). Although these children attended school together, discourses of race positioned Negroes as inferior to whites (Frankenberg, 1994). Much discrimination and prejudice was directed against Negro students in these schools. In many communities, Negroes took it upon themselves to organize segregated schools so that their children could learn in supportive and nurturing environments (Banks, 1995; Brooks, 1990). These Negro communities funded their own schools and hired their own teachers.

In the South, as in the North, discourses of race and class intertwined to limit education for children other than those of the white wealthy class. Education was believed to be a privilege reserved for the white plantation owners. Planters did not advocate the education of the white laborers because they feared that they would become difficult to control. The white laborers themselves believed that education was a privilege reserved for the upper classes, and they accepted their lower status in society (Anderson, 1988; DuBois, 1935). Laborers attempted to move into the upper class by working towards becoming slaveholders.

The Negroes were the first group in the South to advocate the establishment of public schools for all children. In the words of W. E. B. DuBois (1935), it was "the black folk, who connected knowledge with power; who believed that education was the stepping stone to wealth and respect, and that wealth, without education, was crippled" (p. 641). Sunday schools, day schools, and private schools were organized by Negroes throughout the South. Even after the education of slaves was made illegal in 1829, clandestine schools continued to operate and essentially laid the foundation for the public school systems that sprung up in the South after the Civil War (Dubois, 1935).

After the Civil War, discourses of race and class continued to position Negroes as inferior to whites on both sides of the Mason-Dixon line. White northern teachers who migrated south in order to teach in Negro schools were harassed and oftentimes had their lives threatened by southern whites. Negro schools in many southern states were burned to the ground. Although Negro children attended some integrated schools in the North, members of the white upper class oversaw the implementation of the curriculum, chose the textbooks that would be used, and controlled the information that would be taught (DuBois, 1935).

The absence of Negro and African history in the school curriculum and in American society in general became a point of contention for African scholars such as W. E. B. DuBois, George Washington Williams, and Carter G. Woodson.

George Washington Williams was the first Negro scholar to undertake the task of writing a comprehensive history of Negroes. His two-volume *History of the Negro Race in America* documented the development of African civilizations, historical events, and contributions of Negro persons.

It was the type of information that Williams chronicled that DuBois found missing in the curriculum of the Negro college. DuBois (1903) argued that the paucity of information about the contributions and accomplishments of their people caused feelings of self-contempt and inferiority to permeate the Negro consciousness. He advocated the inclusion of Negro history in all universities, especially those that were run by and for Negroes. Consider the following quotation:

> The foundations of knowledge in this race, as in others, must be sunk deep in the college and the university if we would build a solid, permanent structure. Internal problems of social advance must inevitably come–problems of work and wages, of families and homes, of morals and the true valuing of the things of life: and all these and other inevitable problems of civilization the Negro must meet and solve largely for himself, by reason of his isolation; and can there be any possible solution other than by study and thought and an appeal to the rich experiences of the past? (1903, p. 89).

Working against discourses of race that positioned Negroes as biologically inferior, DuBois believed that emphasizing Negro accomplishments would not only instill a greater sense of pride in Negroes themselves but would also illustrate to whites the contributions that Negroes had made in the world and in American society. He and his fellow Negro scholars believed that once whites were made aware of the achievements of Negroes, they would grant them full participation in American society (DuBois, 1935).

World War I brought a sense of hope and renewal to the Negro people. The notion that Negroes could become full participants in American society, for the first time, seemed to be an attainable goal. The number of war-related jobs in the North was growing too rapidly for the existing labor market there. Companies sent recruiters to southern states with promises of better economic and job opportunities in the North. Large numbers of Negroes migrated to the North and did indeed find the conditions the recruiters had promised. Yet as blacks began to settle into city neighborhoods, whites resisted their presence. Neighborhoods, schools, and workplaces became racial battlegrounds (Takaki, 1993).

The work of Carter G. Woodson echoed that of DuBois. Woodson (1933) charged that the public schools in America mis-educated the Negro. Negro students were taught about the achievements of peoples such as the Greeks and Romans, yet the historical accomplishments of the Africans were completely overlooked. At the time Woodson published *The Mis-education of the Negro* (1933), only eighteen high schools in the entire country were reported as offering any type of course on Negro history. Woodson argued this ignorance of Negro history allowed whites to define the parameters of schooling for the benefit of their own children. Woodson asserted:

> The same educational process which inspires and stimulates the oppressor with the thought that he is worth everything and has accomplished everything worth while, depresses and crushes at the same time the spark of genius in the Negro by making him feel that his race does not amount to much and never will measure up to the standards of other peoples. The Negro thus educated is a hopeless liability of the race. (1933, p. xiii)

Although most Negro educators agreed that Negro history should be taught at the university level, many argued against introducing issues of race to elementary-aged children. They believed to do so would prematurely expose children to racism and discrimination. Woodson (1933) countered by arguing that Negro children experienced race on a daily basis and that the older children got, the more difficult it was to change attitudes and opinions. In 1926, Woodson created Negro History Week for elementary school children and in 1937 he founded the *Negro History Bulletin,* which published material for teachers to use with elementary and secondary school students.

Yet even as Woodson advocated the teaching of Negro subjects, he also expressed his doubts about the ability of the teaching force to carry out this task. According to Woodson, teachers had been subjected to years of schooling in which they were mis-educated. He contended that a restructuring of the whole system of education would lead to freedom and independence and that teachers, both Negro and white, would lead the way to revolutionizing the social order (Woodson, 1933).

Discourses of Harmony, Understanding, and Acceptance

> But the problem (discrimination) is essentially an educational problem, since all the prejudices involved in it have been acquired by each individual during his lifetime. And if these have been learned, it is an educational problem as to whether any more such shall be learned, and whether present ones may not be unlearned. What will be so learned or unlearned depends largely on what the school, working in cooperation with the home and community, attempts to do. (Vickery and Cole, 1943)

As the forces of World War II swept through America, social and economic conditions rapidly changed. An abundance of war-related factory jobs available in the Northern states led to another influx of Southern blacks, poor rural whites, and Mexican Americans (Banks, 1995; Takaki, 1993). Northern neighborhoods overflowed with a diversity of peoples vying for employment and housing opportunities. Discourses of race and class continued to position whites in positions of power. Race riots erupted in urban centers. This increase in racial and ethnic tension, coupled with the growing feelings of mistrust directed towards

Jewish and Japanese Americans, led to religious and ethnic conflicts as well (Takaki, 1993). One response to these growing tensions was the development of intercultural education, an initiative created by a group of mainly white liberals who argued that education was one way to alleviate the ethnic, religious, socioeconomic, and racial tensions that were building in America (Banks, 1995; Cole, 1945; Cook, 1947; Olneck, 1990; Vickery & Cole, 1943).

Intercultural education rejected the ideologies of assimilation and cultural pluralism and embraced the notion of cultural democracy (Cole, 1945). Advocates of cultural democracy believed that there was room within mainstream American society to acknowledge and appreciate the cultures of all minority groups. In the words of Vickery and Cole, "All citizens will understand, appreciate and support both the principle of majority rule and the principle of minority rights, so that neither will become all-powerful at the expense of the other, thus threatening our form of government" (1943, p. 33).

The public schools were targeted as the primary vehicles for transmitting this information to children while the Bureau for Intercultural Education sponsored radio programs with such titles as "Americans All–Immigrants All" to bring the message of cultural democracy to adults (Cole, 1945; Vickery & Cole, 1943). Adult education courses were also designed, and community and religious groups were established to promote "good racial and cultural feelings" as well as "moral consistency" in social behavior (Cole, 1945).

Teachers were advised to teach children to act with "unswerving loyalty" and to aspire to "democratic ideals" (Vickery & Cole, 1943, p. 43). This was to be accomplished through a variety of teaching methods. According to Vickery and Cole, teachers presented children with activities such as listening to music and folk tales and viewing artwork and handicrafts from minority groups, prior to teaching facts and information that addressed racial, ethnic, religious, and socioeconomic issues. Teachers were also advised to provide opportunities for minority and majority students to work cooperatively both in and out of school. Students were taught to think critically about the discrimination and racism that permeated the culture and were urged to "look behind supposed innate characteristics to understand differences in group behavior" while reflecting on their own behavior and actions towards others.

Discourses of cultural democracy entwined with discourses of gender, positioning female teachers as preservers of American unity and democracy. For example, it was the job of the early childhood teacher to teach issues of social living. This included giving "special attention to the manners and morals of all children whose home training is inadequate in order to correct the faults to which the established majority group legitimately objects" (Vickery & Cole, 1943, p. 88). In other words, it was the job of the teacher to indoctrinate the young immigrant and Negro children in her care with the behaviors of the dominant culture.

The discourses of race that surged in and through the genre of multicultural education during this era were color and power evasive (Frankenberg, 1994). This discursive approach highlighted the heritage and contributions of particular groups, but it completely disregarded issues of power and white superiority that permeated American society (Olneck, 1990). Racial, ethnic, religious, and socioeconomic hierarchies remained intact. Discourses of race commingled with discourses of class and religion to construct all Americans as being alike while at the same moment highlighting selective differences. These selective differences, expressed in artwork, music, food, and the celebration of holidays, were to be appreciated by all Americans.

Discourses of cultural democracy placed the focus on changing individual attitudes and behaviors rather than addressing group inequities. This focus was so deeply ingrained in the intercultural movement that children were often given pre- and post- tests to measure changes in their thinking after completing designated units of study (Olneck, 1990). The emphasis on the individual is also evident in the appearance of the term "intercultural education," which evolved into "intergroup education" and by the 1950s into "human relations" (Olneck, 1990).

Discourses of Black and Ethnic Power

Black History is refusal to give over our lives, our creativity, our history, our future into the hands of white America, for those hands have proved themselves totally inadequate and ultimately dangerous. So we demand hegemony over our institutions. We seek the control of telling our story. Negro History Week becomes passé, for we move toward controlling the total definition of society. Racial pride becomes Black consciousness, no longer focused on how we look to the white world, but centered on our preparedness to move for a new world. (Vincent Harding, director of the Institute of the Black World, 1970, p. 27)

After World War II disillusionment and a sense of betrayal crept through the Negro community. Many Negro soldiers returned from a war fought against fascism and racism only to find that segregationist policies still persisted in the United States. Legal discourses, such as those surrounding *Brown v. Board of Education*, which declared segregated schools to be unconstitutional, promoted language that was equitable. These legal discourses provided ammunition to those who sought group rights and inspired a group of black intellectuals and activists to push for social equality. They promoted a nonviolent approach to social activism and orchestrated bus boycotts, sit-ins, freedom rides, and marches to get their message across to the American public.

Socioeconomic and generational discourses collided with one another as young blacks, to the surprise of their seniors, organized their own agenda for advancing equality–Black power and racial pride. Young blacks advanced a more assertive type of social activism and demanded "restitution for generations of oppression, racism and cultural imperialism" (Gay, 1983b, p. 560). Although both of these movements fought for equity in areas such as transportation, housing, and police conduct, much of their focus was on school desegregation. Black students argued not only for the desegregation of schooling but also for the implementation of black studies programs in their schools. Discourses of race consciousness and race pride became entwined with discourses of black power as students argued for the inclusion of black history taught from a black perspective. Discourses of black power positioned blacks as contributors to an American society with a story that was waiting to be told. They contended that the America portrayed in mainstream textbooks and history courses had never really existed (Gay, 1983a; Harding, 1970). In the words of Vincent Harding:

> ... the majority of us who struggled accepted the idea that the myth of American democracy was a great truth—except for us—but we also accepted on various levels of our consciousness the fact that only a minority of us would actually make it into the mainstream. For only a minority was "ready" for integration at any given time as the keepers of the society defined "readiness." (1970, p. 3)

Black students believed that a reinterpretation of history that exposed the deliberate omissions and toppled the racist assumptions upon which the school curricula were built would lead to a new sense of personal identity and liberation. Students rallied for black studies courses in literature, sociology, psychology, political science, music, and African languages as well as history (Ford, 1973).

Discourses of black power and the Civil Rights Movement in the United States became entwined with discourses of anticolonialism that rippled throughout the world. American blacks aligned their status in the United States with the peoples of Africa, Asia, and Latin America who were struggling toward liberation from their colonial oppressors. Embedded in the ideology of the black power movement were notions of separatism, self-determination, and liberation (Harding, 1970). Discourses of black power generated a new sense of racial awareness both nationally and internationally.

Frankenberg (1994) refers to the discourses that grew out of the Civil Rights Movement as discourses of race cognizance. These discourses were alternatives to the deeply entrenched discourses of color and power evasion. Discourses of race cognizance positioned race as a major factor in the shaping of one's perspectives, opportunities, practices, and daily life. As Frankenberg contends:

> Race cognizance articulates explicitly the contradiction that racism represents: on the one hand, it acknowledges the existence of racial inequality and white privilege and on the other, does not lean on ontological or essential difference in order to justify inequality or explain it away. (p. 160)

Discourses of race cognizance spread throughout the United States and surrounded a variety of ethnic groups. Mexican Americans, Puerto Ricans, Asian Americans, Native Americans, and others became actively involved in collective struggles for economic and political power. These groups, too, attempted to reclaim their pasts by challenging the status quo. Ethnic groups, taking the lead from their black counterparts, argued for structural changes in schools and advocated ethnic studies programs. School policies and politics began to change: teaching forces were created that included minority staff members; ethnic and racial learning styles and patterns of behavior were encouraged; diverse languages and dialects were introduced to the students and sanctioned by the school; testing and counseling programs were reevaluated, and community involvement in the schools was encouraged (Banks, 1981).

Discourses of Multicultural Education

Children have the right to their own language, their own culture. We must fight cultural hegemony and fight the system by insisting that children be allowed to express themselves in their own language style. It is not they, the children, who must change, but the schools. To push children to do anything else is repressive and reactionary. (Delpit, 1995, p. 37)

As black and ethnic studies programs matured, advocates pushed for these programs to be integrated into existing school curricula rather than offered as extra courses. Students were provided with a "more realistic and relevant curriculum" that took into account societal diversity as well as the need for a cognitive base on which to build an understanding of the ethnic and racial minorities who have helped to shape the United States (Forester, 1982, p. 121). By the early 1970s white ethnic studies programs had been initiated by such groups as Italians, Germans, Poles, and Jews. The term "multiethnic" emerged as a variety of ethnic studies programs were incorporated into the mainstream curriculum.

A multiethnic ideology maintains that in the creation of America, minority groups influenced the dominant culture just as the dominant culture influenced minority groups (Banks, 1981). Further, Banks argues that Americans negotiate on a daily basis among and within several cultures. This recognition leads to one of the major objectives of multiethnic education: to "help students develop cross-cultural competency, consisting of the skills, attitudes, and abilities needed to function within their own ethnic subsociety and the universal American culture, as well as within and across different ethnic cultures" (Banks, 1981, p. 21). Advocates of multiethnic education support the notion that all students, including those in the majority, would benefit from being taught about the contributions, histories, and cultures of various ethnic groups.

As multiethnic education developed, a variety of other cultural groups fought for inclusion in the curriculum as well. Women, the handicapped, the poor, and the aged demanded that their contributions and histories be recognized and that their specific interests be served (Gay, 1983a). Multiethnic education evolved into "education that is multicultural" (Gay, 1983a; Gollnick and Chinn, 1986; Grant, 1977, 1978).

Carl Grant was the first educational scholar to promote education that is multicultural as opposed to multicultural education. Grant (1978) argued that "education that is multicultural" was a comprehensive, integrated term that necessitated changes in the educational system as a whole. According to Grant (1978), these changes included creating faculties that reflect the diversity present in American society, developing curricula that address the contributions and histories of all cultural groups, acknowledging that languages, values, and belief systems of groups are different not deficient, and promoting the use of textbooks and materials that are inclusive and free of bias. These changes, implemented nationwide, would lead to the affirmation and respect of all types of diversity.

By the mid-1980s multicultural education had permeated school curricula across the country. Although the intent of multicultural education was to challenge the status quo, many schools stopped short of the more emancipatory goals. Sleeter and Grant (1994) have identified some approaches to multicultural education, such as those attached to the discourse of difference, that actually work against the promotion of equity and social justice. Within the discourse of difference, members of nondominant cultures are perceived as needing to be assimilated into the dominant culture in order to be successful in U.S. schools and society. Although children from nondominant cultures are viewed as bringing strengths into the classroom which can be built upon, the main goal of the teacher is to assimilate these children into the dominant culture. While the home culture is honored, the main objective of education is to teach children a "standard body of knowledge and set of values and skills that all American children need to acquire" (Sleeter & Grant, 1994, p. 52).

Critics of multicultural education also emerged at this time. The United States was experiencing a backlash against the gains made by members of nondominant groups during the 1960s and 1970s. The notion gained currency that oppressed groups had been adequately compensated for earlier acts of prejudice and discrimination and were now receiving more than their share of economic and social support. This prompted rallies against policies and programs such as affirmative action. This conservative backlash spread through all sectors of society, including the schools, and redefined the genre of multicultural education.

At the present moment, several distinct discourses flowing in and through the genre of multicultural education can be identified. Many groups continue to promote multicultural education in a variety of forms, but conservative groups have successfully appropriated and subverted some of the discourses attached to the

Civil Rights Movement (McLaren, 1994). Drawing on the discourse of cultural democracy prevalent during the intercultural movement, these conservative groups promote a common culture that is monolingual, based on the values of the white middle class, and defends the teaching of a Western base of knowledge (McCarthy, 1993; McLaren, 1994).

Although conservative discourses of multicultural education would appear to be the most damaging to the multicultural movement, the appropriation of the discourses of race pride, race consciousness, and racial power into the dominant discourse has also served to weaken the original intentions of multicultural education. Debates over issues of representation, values, and attitudes have overshadowed the demand for structural changes in education and the critique of Eurocentric forms of education that were embedded in the Civil Rights Movement. McCarthy (1993) has identified three categories of discourses that, along with discourses of conservatism, currently define the genre of multicultural education. He refers to these as *discourses of cultural understanding, discourses of cultural competence,* and *discourses of cultural emancipation.*

Discourses of cultural understanding contain remnants of the discourses of cultural democracy that swirled around the intercultural movement. Today those drawing on discourses of cultural understanding promote similar notions. Discourses of cultural understanding position all individuals as being equal. Acceptance and respect of individual differences are promoted as well as the notion that deep down inside we are really all the same. Individuals drawing on discourses of cultural understanding believe that, through better communication and changes in attitudes, harmonious relationships will be formed between and among diverse groups of people.

Discourses of cultural competence promote an ideology of cultural pluralism. Discourses of cultural competence position all students as needing to be bilingual and to learn about ethnic studies in order to participate fully in American society. The aim is to maintain cultural diversity, particularly the language and identity of nondominant groups (McCarthy, 1993, p. 292). Those who promote the ideology of cultural competence, like those advocating cultural understanding, believe that through developing a better understanding of ethnic diversity, students will experience attitude changes which will reduce discrimination and prejudice.

Discourses of cultural emancipation contain traces of the discourses of black consciousness, black pride, and black power. The ideologies embedded in discourses of cultural emancipation promote a curriculum that includes information about the contributions and histories of nondominant cultural groups in order to create educational experiences at school that are more consonant with home and community experiences. Those advocating an ideology of cultural emancipation contend that the level of academic success of students of nondominant cultures will be elevated once schools become more meaningful and relevant to them. This academic success will lead, in turn, to greater economic gains as students enter the job market fully prepared to become contributing members of society.

A discourse of *critical multiculturalism* (McCarthy, 1993; McLaren, 1994) has also emerged. The discourse of critical multiculturalism is infused with ideologies of black power. This discourse attempts to highlight the connections between knowledge and power and opposes the global imposition of values considered "Western." Discourses of critical multiculturalism merge with discourses of race and class to position all students at the center of their own educational experience. According to McLaren (1994), teachers need to build alliances that will work against the institutional racism that is entrenched in schools. Voices of the members of the nondominant culture need to be affirmed, and teachers need to create spaces for multiple voices and perspectives in the classroom.

Discourses of multicultural education work against the ideology of a universal child (who is white and middle class) and position children and families of nondominant cultures as having backgrounds, needs, and experiences that are different from those of their white counterparts. This chapter has identified a succession of educational reform efforts directed towards meeting the needs of the children and families of nondominant cultural groups. Teachers are positioned as the revolutionaries of the educational system.

The next chapter discusses the Equity Academy, a teacher education program that focuses on issues of diversity and social justice. It is from this program the first-year first-grade teacher, Ms. Gonzales, has been graduated.

CHAPTER SEVEN

A Multicultural Teacher Education Program

In the summer of 1993, the Equity Academy (EA) was implemented as a three-year experimental graduate program in Elementary Education in the Department of Curriculum and Instruction at Midwestern University. Prospective teachers who successfully complete the EA are graduated with a masters degree in education and receive certification to teach first through sixth grades. Prospective teachers in the EA are required to complete 39 credit hours of course work, conduct a master's research project, and pass a comprehensive examination.

The emphasis of the EA, as its name suggests, centers on preparing elementary educators to teach children from all ethnic, racial, and socioeconomic backgrounds. The program also incorporates a variety of other educational reforms, such as the introduction of an integrated curriculum, the promotion of reflective practice, the use of action research, and collaborative efforts between the university and elementary schools. Professor Kurt Meyer, one of the creators of the EA program, explains, "the hope was that [the EA], like the National Teacher Corps, would light a variety of reform initiatives in different places."

The EA was created in response to the concern on the part of some faculty members that the needs of children of color were not being addressed in the undergraduate Elementary Education Program. A second concern was that no initial teaching certification program existed for graduate students whose baccalaureate degrees were in fields other than teaching, but who chose to enter the field of teaching. The creators of the EA envisioned it as a small program within the larger Elementary Education Program. The EA faculty wanted particularly to recruit graduate students of color into the program. The graduate status of the program would allow faculty to conduct a national search that they believed would help them attract a diverse population.

The EA spans a 15-month period, which is consistent with the length of other masters degree programs nationally and at Midwestern. For the graduate students who are admitted into the EA, course work begins in the summer. During the fall semester, prospective teachers take courses as they participate in a student teaching practicum three days a week. In the spring, prospective teachers are enrolled in one course as they complete their final student teaching experience.

The Equity Academy

One of the major reform initiatives of the EA is a commitment to a close collaboration between the university and the elementary schools. According to Dr. Meyer, the idea is to "break down the barriers between the school and the University and somehow integrate academic knowledge and practitioner knowledge more closely." University and elementary school educators collaborate on many facets of the EA. Together, they choose the graduate students who are to be admitted, develop the methods courses, and plan student teaching experiences.

In order to be chosen for involvement in the EA, elementary schools have to meet two requirements. In the words of Dr. Charo Sanchez, who co-directs the EA with Dr. Ellen Jackson, "we asked people to work with us and required that a third of the staff had to be interested in working on enacting multicultural education, and you had to have a fairly significant population of students of color." At the time of this study, prospective teachers were placed in three elementary schools and one middle school. The program is implemented differently in each of the participating schools. For example, the faculty at Landmere Elementary decided to designate one of their teachers as a half-time on-site supervisor for the EA. Hilltop Elementary, on the other hand, chose to rely on university personnel to carry out the supervision of the prospective teachers in their school.

Each cohort group in the EA consists of approximately 25 individuals who move through their course work together. This large cohort is further divided into three smaller cohorts, each of which is placed at a single school for field placements and student teaching experiences. These small cohorts attend the concurrent practicum and student teaching seminar which is under the guidance of Dr. Jackson, Dr. Sanchez, and Dr. Meyer. Dr. Jackson explained why the cohorts are organized in this manner:

> . . . the cohort is important. We're saying that teaching is in a social context, that it matters where you are and who you're with, if it's not a sort of generic technical skill, then we have to give prospective teachers the opportunity to develop in that social context. . . . To bring together eight people who are together already, there are different kinds of conversations; there are different ways to look at problems. They can go into each other's rooms. They often work with each other's kids. They are much more a part of the school community than they are wedded to a classroom.

According to Dr. Jackson, the notion of the cohort is important because in the EA, teaching is conceptualized as being a collaborative enterprise rather than a solitary venture. Placing the small cohort groups together in the same educational setting allows prospective teachers to form a community in which they can continue conversations, observations, and insights that are born in their individual practices. In this context, relationships are built on the shared knowledge that grows out of the communal and individual experiences of teaching.

Another level of university and elementary school collaboration is visible in the way that curriculum is integrated to shape the teaching methods courses. Committees of university and elementary school faculty work together to create courses that transcend disciplinary boundaries. Evidence of the blending of content areas can be seen in the course titles listed in Table 7.1. For example, one of the methods courses, "Workshop in School Program Development: Literacy and the Arts," includes content material that is explored through conventional methodology as well as through music, art, dance, and creative dramatics. Because methods courses have been created across disciplinary boundaries, they are often team-taught by university faculty members.

The integrated curriculum is only one way that teacher educators in the EA attempt to "redefine the notion of method." The methods courses differ from those advocated in more teacher education programs in other ways as well. Dr. Jackson, referring to the work of Gitlin and Bullough, explains that the EA faculty encourages its students to "become students of teaching," rather than promoting a more traditional "performative" approach. Dr. Jackson said:

> I want prospective teachers to understand teaching methods as an intellectual activity, a political activity. And to think about the ways in which they intellectually are engaged in it and in intellectually challenging students. So I want them to think hard, and I want them to help kids think hard. I want them to understand that they are engaged in some political activity, either inducting them into the current system as it is or helping them change. Those are for me some pretty clear choices that people can make.

The EA promotes the idea that teaching methodologies need to be assessed continuously in light of their ability to provide cultural currency for all children. Dr. Jackson wants prospective teachers to understand that what and how they choose to teach either inducts children into the culture of power or excludes them from it.

Dr. Sanchez echoes this emphasis on teaching as a political act and the notion that prospective teachers have the ability to provide all children with the skills to negotiate within the culture of power. She describes the EA in the following manner:

> What the EA means to me is teaching for social justice and equity, opening up opportunities for all children in classrooms to have higher expectations in learning the content of the curriculum, and teaching children to be critical inquirers and knowledge makers in the classroom.

From her perspective, although children receive the skills to negotiate within the culture of power that surrounds schools, the personal knowledge that they bring to school is honored and valued as well. Prospective teachers work toward issues of social justice and equity in classrooms and society by constructing all children as knowers rather than just those who come equipped with the white middle-class ways of knowing.

This emphasis on social justice and equity was visible in all of my conversations with faculty and in all of their course syllabi. Faculty and graduate students within C&I teach the majority of the courses. The listing of the courses and the sequence in which prospective teachers are required to complete their course work are listed in Table 7.1.

Faculty and staff members who were affiliated with the EA consistently expressed their mission as one of preparing teachers to work towards change, understand issues of diversity, become reflective teachers, and work collaboratively with one another. The teacher educators in the EA often utilized different methods and strategies within their practice, but the meanings of the themes they were promoting were consistent. Working within a multicultural social reconstructionist discourse, the faculty and staff in the EA held a common vision for teachers and, ultimately, for children.

The discourses of multiculturalism and social reconstructionism have their roots firmly planted in the long historical tradition of scholars working within a critical perspective at Midwestern. Within this discourse, society is conceptualized as in need of re-ordering so that it better serves the interests of all people, especially those who are members of nondominant cultural groups (Sleeter and Grant, 1994). Children are believed to be future citizens who can choose to work for structural change in society. The idea is that children need to be prepared to

TABLE 7.1 Professional Sequence of Courses Taken in the Equity Academy

Summer	Teaching and Diversity (C&I)
	Culture, Curriculum & Learning (C&I)
	Independent Field Work (C&I)
Fall	Workshop in School Program Development: Social Studies, Physical Education & Health Education (C&I)
	Workshop in School Program Development: Literacy and the Arts (C&I)
	Workshop in Program Development: Science, Mathematics & Environmental Education (C&I)
	Workshop in School Program Development: Field Experiences
Spring	Strategies for Inclusive Schooling (C&I)
	Independent Field Work (C&I)
Summer	Social Issues in Education (EPS)
	Human Development in Infancy and Early Childhood (Ed. Psych.)
	Research and Thesis (C&I)

think critically and work collectively so that they can engage in activities that promote social change. Positioned within this discourse, prospective teachers are responsible for directly addressing issues of diversity in the classroom. Issues of race, class, gender, sexual orientation, and socioeconomic status are questioned and critiqued. Teachers encourage children to examine their "own lives in order to develop their practical consciousness about real injustices in society and to develop constructive responses" (Sleeter & Grant, 1994, p. 225).

Constructing the Meaning of Change

Three of the four themes that predominate in the EA–diversity, reflective teaching, and collaboration–are consistent with three of the themes highlighted in the EEP. Because the EA and the EEP both employ faculty who work within C&I these parallels make sense. The fourth and most prominent theme emphasized in the EA is change.

Teacher educators in the EA use the terms "change" and "transformation" interchangeably. Dr. Jackson identifies personal transformation as one of the most important components of the EA. As she explains, "What we try to do in the program is force the transformation. Now some of the people come to us already having gone through something . . . but we try to highlight [transformation] as part of the program." She went on to explain how teacher educators in the EA create situations that make teachers "ripe" for transformation. One of the aspects of the program that provides transformative opportunities is the extended contact prospective teachers are able to have with the students and families with whom they work. Prospective teachers often meet their students in the summer as they carry out their community volunteer work. In the fall, student interns in Dr. Jackson's cohort begin their field placements in one classroom setting and complete their student teaching in the same classroom in the spring. Dr. Jackson said:

> So one of the things that I think is the right thing to do is to place people in a setting over time so they essentially are in their settings about a year, the nine or ten school months. But there's also summer, that many of them have been right there in the community in the volunteer aspect of it. And they see so many changes, see so much occurring. And so because they're a part of the change, and kids change quickly, because they are part of the kids changing, I think that's an environment that's ripe for transformation.

In Dr. Jackson's opinion, this sustained interaction with children in the classroom setting, coupled with the interactions that occur with their families outside of school, can move teachers to new understandings. As children change over time so do those teachers who have allowed themselves to be "in relation" with children and families. Prospective teachers are provided with the opportunity to invest themselves personally in the relationships they are building over time. Through this personal investment, prospective teachers come to see themselves as intimately involved in the process of change they see occurring in children. From Dr. Jackson's perspective, transformations are revelations about the self that are always inextricably tied to social relationships. Transformation occurs when there is a shift in the way prospective teachers think about themselves and their teaching.

Ms. Dee Reynolds, a graduate student, is responsible for supervising prospective teachers in their field placements and in their final student teaching experiences as well as co-teaching a student teaching seminar with Dr. Sanchez. Ms. Reynolds explains one of the goals that she has for the six prospective teachers with whom she works:

> I want my students to name things. For example, when my students go into a school and they have all these special programs, these pull-out programs for children, I want them to look at why they're doing that and how we're keeping the status quo by maintaining those kinds of programs. I'm not saying that they can go into the schools and change everything, but I want them to question those kinds of things so we quit killing our poor children, our children of color, and our white kids who leave thinking they are so wonderful. So mainly talk is action for me and that does mean change. We need to talk about how we can make changes in the way that we deal with all of our children.

Change in this context refers to alterations in the ways of speaking, thinking, and acting that can occur through dialogue with others. From the perspective of Ms. Reynolds, dialogue can lead to new levels of awareness as the silences in schools which circumscribe issues of diversity are broken.

Both Ms. Reynolds and Dr. Jackson hope that transformations in the ways that prospective teachers think about themselves and their teaching will lead to changes in schooling which are more equitable and just. Dr. Sanchez even refers to prospective teachers as "change agents." She explains her hope that, through their participation in the community service aspect of the EA, prospective teachers will become change agents in the school.

Once a week, prospective teachers eat dinner at Hebron House, a community facility that provides meals for needy families. The prospective teachers attend the meal as hosts and eat with the families rather than simply serving them. The power relationship between served and servers is altered as prospective teachers and community members dine together. Dr. Sanchez explains what she wants prospective teachers to take from this experience:

> ... a sense of being a change agent but also as a community member. Someone who develops a caring relationship with children and potentially their families that goes beyond this, "aren't you deprived and let's fix them up" notion. A sense that they are curriculum makers and that through the curriculum, ideologies are lived out. That what you choose to teach comes out of both your personal ideology and those of the power and authority

of the school community. And that there are choices to be made and those choices are critical for you to make carefully . . . I want them to see themselves as able to make changes within a system which will positively benefit kids.

In order to be responsive to the communities in which their children live, prospective teachers need to understand the cultural context of their children's experiences. Dr. Sanchez wants teachers to understand that they are the creators of the curriculum and that they have the power to make pedagogical choices which are inclusive of all of their children's life experiences. Part of that inclusiveness is based on their familiarity with and acceptance of the families of the children whom they teach. Incorporating all of the children's ways of knowing, speaking, and acting within the classroom leads to changes in pedagogical practices that attempt to be inclusive of all children.

Dr. Sanchez, Dr. Jackson, and Ms. Reynolds believe that the extended teaching placements, the community experience, and the provision of opportunities for dialogue can lead to change and transformation in the way that prospective teachers think about themselves and their teaching. These teacher educators also advocate that opportunities for change and transformation be extended to young children.

Positioned within a multicultural social reconstructionist discourse, prospective teachers are immersed in the perspectives, values, and beliefs being promoted in the EA, and this immersion shapes them in very particular ways. They are involved in social practices that expose them to ways of speaking, acting, and interacting that are drawn upon by children and families who are members of nondominant cultures. Developing an understanding of the cultural backgrounds of their students allows prospective teachers to draw on the children's ways of knowing as they create curriculum and carry out instruction in their own classrooms.

Constructing the Meaning of Diversity

The theme of diversity was prominent in all of the conversations that I had with faculty and staff and in all of the course syllabi. The term "diversity" collectively refers to a range of issues including class, race, gender, sexual orientation, physical ability, and religion. Within a multicultural social reconstructionist discourse, these issues are conceived of as social constructions that privilege certain groups of individuals and oppress others. Social inequalities exist because of the way that particular groups of people have been constructed.

In their initial course prospective teachers are introduced to readings that work to destabilize their notions of race, class, gender, and sexual orientation. Readings such as *Social Postmodernism, Beyond Identity Politics* (Nicholson & Steidman, 1995) and *Race, Identity and Representation* (McCarthy & Crichlow,

1993) force prospective teachers to examine how issues of diversity have been constructed. Through readings and discussions, prospective teachers are immediately situated as participants in the maintenance of these constructs that lead to the oppression of nondominant cultural groups. As participants in an unjust system, they are forced to examine how their actions either maintain or disrupt the hegemonic forces that surround schools and society. From this perspective, the role of the teacher is to create an equitable environment in the classroom. One of the ways that this can be done is by drawing on alternative pedagogies.

One instructor, Nancy Rodriguez, begins her course by asking prospective teachers to examine who they are in terms of literacy by writing "literacy autobiographies." As they share these, prospective teachers become more aware of how literacy has been defined in their personal lives. According to Ms. Rodriguez, this exercise helps teachers "unpack the assumptions that they have about literacy and children" from nondominant cultures.

After prospective teachers examine their personal literacy histories, they read about "indigenous literacies" that have grown out of specific communities. For example, prospective teachers read about and discuss how literacy was denied to slaves in the antebellum south. They also read the work of Guadalupe Valdez, who explores how first-generation Mexican immigrant families negotiate multiple systems of literacy. In Ms. Rodriguez's words:

> The unit that we looked at was for families and how they are not at a deficit. That there's a lot of strengths in families and that we have to think about how we're looking at kids from our own specific assumptions, maybe from Eurocentric ways . . . I wanted everything to gravitate from issues of race, class, and gender that dealt with indigenous literacies in communities. Then we would deal with reading, writing, penmanship, and the arts.

Ms. Rodriguez contests the traditional Eurocentric canon by placing the literacies of nondominant cultural groups at the center of her instruction. Through readings and discussions Ms. Rodriguez helps prospective teachers to become aware of how literacy is socially, culturally, politically, and historically situated. Through the creation of literacy autobiographies, she helps to make students aware of the limits of their own personal concepts of literacy.

Ms. Rodriguez honors indigenous literacies such as storytelling in the university classroom. Yet she also makes it clear to prospective teachers that it is their responsibility to teach all of the children in their care to read. She spends a few class sessions lecturing about theories for teaching literacy. As she says, "I want them to understand who created the theory that is seen in the writing processes that are used in elementary schools . . . I want them to have those tools, those words, those codes." By presenting the literacy course in this way, Ms. Rodriguez models the practice of honoring knowledge brought to the classroom while teaching the skills necessary to function successfully in the dominant culture.

Constructing the Meaning of Reflective Teaching

Reflective teaching is a theme that is woven throughout every aspect of the EA. Within a multicultural, social reconstructionist discourse, the term "reflection" is defined as the act of critically and systematically deliberating on one's actions in collaboration with others. One of the ways that Dr. Sanchez and the other teacher educators in the EA promote reflection is by engaging prospective teachers in the sharing of teaching stories. Prospective teachers are asked to write stories about their practice and reflect on how their race, class, gender, sexual orientation, and language background shape the way they approach their teaching and at the, same time, provide or constrain possibilities for children. Ms. Reynolds explains:

> The seminar was really a space for people to share their teaching stories in different ways, so people got used to the whole process of reflecting critically upon what they were doing. They talked about when they fell flat on their faces. So that we could all learn from that and help each other. As people told their stories, Dr. Sanchez would always steer them back to looking at their teaching and looking at their children, always highlighting issues of race, class, gender, and sexuality.

Dr. Sanchez continually ties the personal teaching stories to issues of race, class, gender, and sexual orientation. By making these connections she keeps the personal tied to the larger social context of schooling. During the process of collaboratively re-examining their practice, prospective teachers are given the opportunity to gain personal insights as well as to challenge the status quo.

Similarly, Dr. Meyer defines "reflective teaching" as an examination of personal and political aspects of teaching. He also speaks about the importance of preparing reflective teachers and discusses how he attempted to engage prospective teachers in reflection:

> I have some clear ideas about the kinds of connections that I would like students to be able to make. I'd like to expose them to different perspectives on issues and to have them think through what their position is rather than adopt any position, including one that I might favor. So it's exposure to certain kinds of issues, the deliberation about alternative perspectives, the recognition of the connection between classroom reality on an everyday basis, and larger issues of equity and social justice.

Dr. Meyer encourages prospective teachers to make connections between their personal classroom experiences and larger issues of equity and social justice. One of the ways that he attempts to help teachers think through these issues is by engaging them in action research. All prospective teachers in Dr. Meyer's class conduct an action research project to meet their masters thesis requirements. These projects are carried out in the classrooms in which prospective teachers are student teaching. In the process, they reflect critically on an issue over time while studying the current academic literature on their topic.

The EA faculty hopes that this systematic reflection will lead to insights that will provoke changes in thought and action. Part of the goal of immersing prospective teachers in action research is to help them understand that what they do on a daily basis in the classroom has social and political ramifications. Through action research, classrooms can become important sites for social change.

Teaching prospective teachers that they have the power to generate knowledge which can inform their work and the work of other educators also encourages these future teachers to work against the status quo. Action research allows teachers to resist top-down reform and to become active participants in school change (Zeichener, 1994). By being involved in these processes of knowledge generation, prospective teachers are working against the hierarchy that privileges university over practitioner knowledge.

Constructing the Meaning of Collaboration

The fourth theme that is promoted by the teacher educators in the EA is collaboration. The term "collaboration" refers to groups of individuals working collectively. In the EA this happens on multiple levels.

The EA is built on a partnership forged between the university and the elementary school. Although representatives from both Midwestern and the elementary schools express a sense that the institutional collaboration is not fully actualized, teacher educators do express a belief that they have learned from one another. An elementary teacher and on-site supervisor of the prospective teachers in the EA says:

> One of the reasons that this staff said yes to being involved in the EA was because they saw it as the potential to be involved as teacher educators. And there were promises of helping design the methods courses, helping teach the methods courses, and it was likely that methods courses would be taught here sometimes too. The reality of what happened was that there were two people from each building selected to go help design methods courses. So there wasn't even a representative from each building for each course.... But there's knowledge of each other's geographic location and that we're in this together as teacher educators. And my assumption of that is, and I think my colleagues share it, is that collaboration improves everyone's practice. From the university campus to the school campus, everyone is learning.

Another level of collaboration that the EA promotes was among the university faculty. The methods courses are often team taught by university faculty members. The student teaching seminars are always co-taught, either by a university faculty member and a graduate assistant or by a faculty member and an on-site elementary school supervisor. Such team teaching challenges the individualistic notions that surround teaching and learning and reinforces the idea that knowledge is socially constructed.

Collaboration is also promoted among the prospective teachers enrolled in the EA. Cohort groups are structured to encourage collaboration and, within the program, reflective teaching is understood to be a cooperative enterprise. A graduate student and teaching assistant who co-directs a student teaching seminar with Dr. Jackson discusses what she hopes the prospective teachers have learned and will take into their future classrooms:

> I want them to continue to learn and teach through dialogue and not to believe that "because I am the teacher, I know everything." [I want them to look] at their children and other professionals as a team, as a member of their team, and continue to teach from the premise that knowledge is basically a collaborative venture.

These comments reinforce the notion that the creation of knowledge is a communal act rather than an individual one.

The Genre of the Equity Academy

A multicultural social reconstructionist discourse permeates the genre of the EA. Embedded within this discourse is a particular ideology that shapes what it means to be a teacher. As prospective teachers are enveloped by the genre of the EA, they begin to appropriate the particular ways of thinking, speaking, acting, and interacting that are carried within this particular discourse. The quotations in Table 7.2 serve to illustrate the themes as they are defined within a sociocultural discourse by the faculty and staff of the EA.

TABLE 7.2 EA Program Themes as Defined Within a Multicultural Social Reconstructionist Discourse

	Multicultural Social Reconstructionist Discourse
Change	"Someone who develops a caring relationship with children and potentially their families that goes beyond this, aren't you deprived and lets fix them up notion. . . . I want them to see themselves as able to make changes within a system which will positively benefit kids."
Diversity	". . . we have to think about how we're looking at kids from our own specific assumptions, maybe from Eurocentric ways . . . I wanted everything to gravitate from the middle that dealt with issues of race, class, and gender that dealt with indigenous literacies in communities. Then we would deal with reading, writing, penmanship, and the arts."
Reflection	"I have some clear ideas about the kinds of connections that I would like students to be able to make. . . . So its exposure to certain kinds of issues, the deliberation about alternative perspectives, the recognition of the connection between classroom reality on an everyday basis, and larger issues of equity and social justice."
Collaboration	"I want them to continue to learn and teach through dialogue and not to believe that 'because I am the teacher, I know everything.' [I want them to look] at their children and other professionals as a team, as a member of their team and continue to teach from the premise that knowledge is basically a collaborative venture."

Prospective teachers in the EA are positioned within a multicultural social reconstructionist discourse as they are placed in student teaching relationships, share teaching stories, and engage in action research projects. As they take on different aspects of the identities that are made available to them, they create possibilities for themselves and for the children and families with whom they work. More specifically, within a multicultural social reconstructionist discourse the EA teacher:

- presents information that helps children to understand that they are part of a larger sociopolitical context.
- acknowledges and builds upon the culture of the students.
- presents curricula that directly address issues of diversity and provides children with strategies to help them work against prejudice and discrimination.
- engages in critical self-examination within a teaching collective
- builds alliances with others to work towards social change.

Constructions of the Prospective Equity Academy Teacher

The teacher educators in the EA describe the prospective teachers currently enrolled in the program as "knowledgeable," "extremely talented," and "committed to issues of social justice." This is not surprising because the standards for admission and continuation in the program are very high. In fact, several teacher educators express pride in the high attrition rate within the program. Dr. Jackson, explaining that 4 of the 21 (19%) prospective teachers who entered the cohort the first year of the program had dropped out, says:

> We don't give them a lot of chances. The program is too intense. I mean we're not heartless. We don't just say "get out" but because the supervision is pretty close when we see the problem, they get called in. We think about ways we might try to solve those problems and if those don't work, we strongly advise that they leave the certification aspect of it. So every year we have people dropping out.

While one of the goals of the EA faculty and staff was to assemble multicultural cohort groups that would become learning communities, attracting people of color to the program has proved to be difficult. Dr. Sanchez explains:

> We have not been able to recruit very many people of color in our program. We are not sure why. There were three per cohort group. Maybe nine out of fifty-some-odd people, maybe 10 percent or 20 percent. I think there are multiple reasons for that.

Dr. Sanchez and others identify several reasons why the program is not acquiring more people of color. One reason is that among the people of color who did apply, several did not meet the admissions criteria. A second reason is that the EA is a full-time graduate program, which automatically excluded those people who had to work to support themselves and/or their families at the same time they pursued a graduate degree. This burden was borne more heavily by students of color. Compounding the problem is the fact that, other than the Advanced Opportunity Fellowships open to all minority graduate students, no scholarships were specifically earmarked for the EA.

The prospective teachers enrolled in the EA, having already completed a first degree, are usually older than the typical novice teacher. They range in age from the mid-twenties through age fifty. Although the cohorts are mixed demographically, the majority of the prospective teachers in the program are described as "white, middle-class females." Dr. Jackson contrasts them with the prospective teachers who are enrolled in the "other" elementary programs:

> There is no profile in the EA. They are that diverse. I can give you a profile of the people in the other programs, because I've taught in the other programs. When I go in there I see young, middle-, lower- to upper-middle-class white females, primarily from [this state], multilingual, able-bodied. . . . Most of the normative categories that we use in this society they'd fit in except that they're women as opposed to men. People who are not like that are the exception. . . . EA students are of course older . . . so age is a difference. We'd like to have more men. The first cohort, a third of the cohort was male. We have not done well with students of color, but we never had a cohort that didn't have some students of color. We've had as many as three African American students this year. We've had Latino students, mixed race students. We've had gay and lesbian students and bilingual students. We had a blind student; she was excellent.

As faculty and staff members discursively construct the prospective teachers with whom they work, they draw on a multicultural social reconstructionist discourse and refer to the high academic expectations that surround the EA. Consider the words of Ms. Rodriguez:

> The way that I see it is that people who have applied for the program have made a serious commitment to issues of social justice, issues of equity, and really thinking about teaching as a practice for social change in schools. So instead of applying to just a regular teaching certification program you're applying to a graduate program, where many of them that come into the program, I wouldn't say all of them, come with different life experiences and different philosophies that they've really reflected on that are real specific toward their commitment with teaching, particularly children of color and children living in poverty. It's a program that I felt was really outstanding regarding the quality of the students you would have.

Another instructor describes one of the cohort groups with whom she has worked:

They were tremendous. They were so enthusiastic, extremely imaginative, conscientious about everything that they did. They simply needed molding and guidance and a little pushing. They always sought out advice with me. They had so much going for them.

The prospective teachers in the EA are described as "committed to social justice," "extremely imaginative," "conscientious," and "intellectually capable." This combination of qualities constructs a very specific image of an elementary school teacher. Through a multicultural social reconstructionist discourse, teacher educators define prospective elementary school teachers as a powerful presence in the field of education. Teachers are positioned as knowledge makers who have the ability to teach and guide children to become creators of knowledge as well. Elementary educators are constructed as having the power to unite with others in the struggle to make schools more just and equitable places to live and work. In the process, teachers also provide children with the skills to negotiate within the dominant culture so that they, too, can join in the struggle towards re-ordering the inequities that are so firmly rooted in U.S. society.

The students who choose to apply to the Equity Academy in essence self select themselves into the program. Although the assumption cannot be made that everyone who enters the program is committed to becoming a change agent, the expectation that they will do so is an explicitly stated goal of the EA. Due to the personal commitments that many of the students bring into the program, the potential for change and transformation may already be in place. Moreover, the teacher educators in the EA believe that the prospective teachers with whom they work are capable of personal transformation and of the type of teaching that allows children to experience a transformation as well.

Chapter 9, examines how this image of an elementary teacher shapes the identities of Ms. Gonzales, a graduate of the EA who teaches first grade at Fernway Elementary School. Chapter 8 discusses the discourses at Fernway Elementary which contribute to the fashioning of Ms. Gonzales' teacher identities. Fernway is in the midst of a number of transitions, including an increase in the number of students of color and an increase in the number of students who are English Language Learners. The staff at Fernway are also attempting to adjust to a new principal who advocates an approach that is uncomfortable for many of the faculty.

CHAPTER EIGHT

Fernway Elementary School

Fernway Elementary School is located on the west side of the city of Mayfield. The neighborhood in which Fernway is located is populated with mid-sized homes built in the early 1950s and 1960s. Although most of the homes are nearly a half century old, they are well maintained, and many are surrounded by attractive landscaping. Nestled among the residences stands the large brick structure of Fernway Elementary. The original building was constructed in 1963, and a new wing was added just last year, which has increased the size of the school considerably. A playground of modest size in the back of the school contains some climbing and sliding equipment. Groups of children use the paved area to play games of foursquare, hopscotch, and tag.

As I enter the side door of Fernway, I stop to look at the new photographs that have been carefully arranged on the bulletin boards on both sides of the hall. The smiling faces of the children who attend Fernway represent a variety of racial and ethnic backgrounds. Ms. Martha Randall, Fernway's principal, is responsible for these photographic displays.

Fernway Elementary is described by the faculty and staff as a school "in transition." Historically, Fernway has served primarily the mainly white middle-class families who resided in the surrounding neighborhood. Although the majority of the children who attend Fernway live in the neighborhood and walk to school, about one fifth of the children are bused in from two outlying areas. The majority of those bused in are children of color who reside in low-income apartment complexes.

Over the course of the past two years, however, the population of children who attend Fernway has shifted dramatically. There are two major reasons for this shift: the growth of subsidized housing in the Fernway neighborhood and the introduction of an English as a Second Language Program at the school.

The introduction of subsidized housing in the neighborhood has led to an increase in the number of children of color and children of low-income families. Ms. Randall explains the situation:

> Well, first of all, the neighborhood that surrounds Fernway used to be what were called starter homes or rental homes. A lot of duplexes. That used to be a great place for people to start out. I don't know if it's the changing economy or what, but that's not a good enough starter home for a lot of people now. Section 8 came in and created places for people who are living in poverty to get a reduced rate, and then they're ensured continual renters, so it's subsidized housing. So there was an increase in subsidized housing and that brought in a lower economic level and poverty, unfortunately. Usually it has a darker face. Usually people of color.

As the number of families who are poor and of color has increased, the number of white middle-class families in the neighborhood has begun to decrease. The school social worker, Marty Paterson, discussing the number of white families moving out of the neighborhood, says, "Just drive through the neighborhood and look at the number of For Sale signs that are posted in people's front yards, and you can get a real good sense of what's happening here." The Fernway neighborhood is experiencing white flight.

Despite the shift in the racial makeup of the children attending Fernway school, the population of children considered white still outnumbers the children of color. Consider the racial/ethnic breakdown of the 484 children enrolled at Fernway as of January 10, 1997: 64 percent white, 1 percent Native American, 15 percent African American, 6 percent Hispanic, and 14 percent Asian (Mayfield School District, Fernway, 1/10/97).

The impact of the increase in subsidized housing that had been occurring over the past several years in the Fernway neighborhood had not been felt so dramatically within the school in the years prior to this time, because many of the children qualified for the English as a Second Language Program. Since there was not an ESL Program at Fernway, this group of mainly Southeast Asian and Latino/Latina children was bused to other schools where their language needs could be met. The new addition to Fernway Elementary provided the space for an ESL program to be located within the school. A first grade teacher discussed how the ESL program had also contributed to the shift in the school population. In her words:

> So a third of our kiddos are on free or reduced lunch. We went from about 9% last year to 33% this year. So there are a lot of needy families. And I think that the English as a Second Language Program has a lot of, I don't know if they are transient families, but a lot of families who come into the neighborhood or move in with a relative and don't have a job and are looking for work. So in the meantime the children would be on free breakfast or free lunch. Not all come for breakfast, but a large majority of them do.

To be exact, 175 of the 484 children at Fernway (36 percent) received free or reduced lunch. According to Ms. Randall, of the 70 children who were ESL students, 99 percent received free or reduced lunch.

This teacher also attributed another new phenomenon at Fernway to the ESL Program: an increase in the mobility of the children and their families. She said, "That mobility is new. . . . We have had more stability in our classrooms in past years." Between the months of November and April, 150 families had moved into the neighborhood while 90 had moved out.

The school psychologist also described Fernway as a school "in transition." She and other faculty members frequently used the terms "diverse" and "diversity" to describe the more heterogeneous population. Diversity in this context referred to the differences in race, gender, socioeconomic status, language, and physical ability. In the words of the school psychologist:

> Oh, I'd say that we just recently have been getting a little bit more diverse because we got our English as a Second Language Program here, and we're getting a few more African American students. We're getting an influx of Hmong students–an influx from Asia–of people moving over to here. They're finding places to live in the neighborhood. . . . So we're getting more and more diverse, and I think that's wonderful because it adds so much richness to what we can learn about people and their differences and different cultures. I think it forces us to see that being different is O.K. and that's why everyone is so special. Because we're all different; we need to get along and all that.

She points to the ESL Program and the influx of Hmong students as well as an increase in the number of African American children as diversifying the student population. From her perspective, this increase in diversity is "wonderful" because it allows the children at Fernway to learn about differences among individuals as well as differences among cultural groups.

The staff members considered the diversity of the Fernway population to be "good," "positive," "exciting," and "something to celebrate." Yet there were tensions surrounding the arrival of this diverse population of students. Many of these tensions were exacerbated by the changes initiated by Ms. Randall when she became principal two years ago.

New Directions for Fernway

Ms. Randall, a white woman, succeeded a white male who had been the principal at Fernway for twelve years prior to her arrival. Over the course of her two years as principal, she has made many changes in the way that things were done. These changes led to friction among groups of staff members as well as friction between staff members and herself.

According to Ms. Randall, upon her arrival at Fernway school she had found an "informal power group." This informal power group had assumed responsibility for making the decisions for all of the staff at Fernway. According to Ms. Randall, her predecessor had failed to deal with the conflicts and confrontations between and among staff members. In the words of Ms. Randall, "He would just sit back and whenever you don't have that type of leadership occurring, a vacuum is created. Whenever you have a vacuum, people fill that vacuum." Ms. Randall took it upon herself to "strip the power and distribute it more equally." Ms. Randall said, "Now we have a legitimate decision-making process that has empowered some people. But when you empower some, you disempower others. It's kind of balanced, but in other ways, that's caused some friction."

In addition to redistributing the power at the school, Ms. Randall attempted to eradicate the racism that she believes surrounds Fernway. Ms. Randall explained:

> There was a level of insensitivity. In fact, some racism. Racism is still here but it was more overt . . . I'm very comfortable with African Americans and probably more sensitive to the problems that they've inherited by being a race that was enslaved. I grew up in the South, and so I grew up when the Martin Luther King riots were occurring. There's a big difference in the North and South. The South, I always thought was real racist, but the North is more racist. . . . Mayfield was very, you know, "Oh yes, we're real advocates for minorities" until they started living in their backyard. Then you started to see middle-class life come out in Mayfield.

Ms. Randall describes Fernway as a school that was racist when she arrived and one in which racism currently persists. She blames the "problems" African American children and families encounter in schooling and society on the fact that their predecessors were slaves. She attributes the inequities that African Americans experience to historical determinism rather than to the hegemonic forces that persist in society today. By defining the problems of African Americans in such a way, Ms. Randall herself practices a form of dysconscious racism (King, 1991) as she fails to make the connection between the racist system in the U.S. that whites continue to maintain for the purpose of promoting domination and subjugation (hooks, 1995).

Nevertheless, as a result of her acknowledgment that inequities do exist in schools, Ms. Randall works to eradicate the practices that she has identified as racist at Fernway. There are three formal ways that she has worked towards this goal. These are (1) creating classes that are mixed racially, economically, and by ability level, (2) supporting the creation of a "minority parent teacher organization," and (3) hiring faculty and staff persons of color.

One of the things Ms. Randall had found most shocking when she began her principalship at Fernway two years ago was the segregation that resulted from the way students were assigned to classes. She said, "When I came here one class in third grade was practically all black. Even black parents commented on it. And the other class was virtually all white and they were all kids of Parent Teacher Organization (PTO) parents." In order to assure integration of gender, ethnicity, and ability in each class, Ms. Randall instituted what she referred to as a "proof of heterogeneity chart."

The proof of heterogeneity chart succeeded in assuring the integration of the classrooms at Fernway, but the parents of the children rarely intermingled with one another. For example, the PTO meetings were run by and attended almost exclusively by white parents. In order to get parents of color involved in the school, Ms. Randall worked with a teacher to organize what she referred to as "minority family nights." According to Ms. Randall, on minority family nights a special guest speaker was invited to specifically address the concerns of parents of color. For example, a district administrator was invited to discuss the issue of achievement. After the formal address and a brief presentation by a group of children, the rest of the meeting was organized so that minority parents and children could socialize with one another. Ms. Randall explained that they had not had any minority parent nights this year because of the expense and because some of the PTO members of the dominant cultural group felt threatened by what they considered to be a form of forced segregation.

The third way that Ms. Randall formally attempted to work against racism was through the hiring of what she referred to as "minority staff" members. The majority of the staff at Fernway was white and female. Ms. Randall explained that, before she joined the staff, the only African American on faculty was the physical education teacher. Since assuming the position of principal at Fernway, she had hired three teachers and three educational assistants. All six of the staff members that Ms. Randall hired were people of color.

Ms. Randall had made a significant number of changes at Fernway in the two years that she had been principal. While some of the Fernway staff members applauded these changes, others expressed serious misgivings. These tensions can be heard in the following two statements by Ms. Knopp and Ms. Beverly Hatfield.

Ms. Katie Knopp, who had taught school for twenty-five years, fourteen of those at Fernway, described the current environment in the following manner:

> Fernway is a neat place to work. I love working with all of the people, all of my cohort. We have a dynamite staff, from music to computer technology to physical education to our educational assistants. All of those people are supportive. . . . We have a lot of new people here this year. We're big. We're growing. Growing pains I call it. . . . You don't know the principal we had before. He was wonderful and a listener, and he trusted us as teachers to do what we felt was best for our classrooms. I don't feel that way with our new administrator. I don't feel that she trusts us. I don't feel that she's always honest. So I feel like I'm walking on eggshells.

From Ms. Knopp's perspective, working at Fernway is wonderful except for the presence of Ms. Randall. She refers to the supportive staff and to the former principal who, she believes, trusted the teachers to do what they felt was best.

Ms. Knopp's description of Fernway and the leadership of Ms. Randall contrasted quite dramatically with that of Ms. Hatfield, one of the new African American teachers that Ms. Randall had recently hired. Although she had taught school for six years prior to her present second-grade teaching position this was Ms. Hatfield's first year at Fernway. Ms. Hatfield described Ms. Randall in the following way:

> Martha has been wonderfully supportive of all kinds of things. She's really big in terms of diversity and encouraging all of these kinds of things to take place. She's been wonderfully supportive of the ideas that I've had and the things that I wanted to do with my students.

Ms. Hatfield specifically mentions Ms. Randall's attention to issues of diversity and the strong support she offers teachers when they address these issues within their classrooms.

As is evident in the words of Ms. Knopp and Ms. Hatfield, the staff at Fernway held conflicting views about Ms. Randall and her management of professional relationships as well as the vision she promoted. The strong personal feelings that many teachers held towards Ms. Randall served to divide the staff. The words of Ms. Knopp and Ms. Hatfield also serve to illustrate the contrast between the views of the teachers who had been at Fernway under the former principal and those who had joined the staff in the past two years. Of the 55 staff members at Fernway school, 20 were in either their first or second year of teaching at Fernway (Fernway document, 2/97). The new teachers had not lived through the history of the school as had those who had been at Fernway for many years. They were not familiar with the policies and practices that had surrounded the school before Ms. Randall arrived. All of these elements led to a staff that was described by Ms. Randall as "fractured." As Ms. Randall said:

> The staff right now I would say is fractured. They have gone through all these changes—students, principal, facility—and it has taken a toll on the group. The dynamics were problematic before all these changes occurred, but it's just kind of brought them to the surface now. There have been quite a few hard feelings among the staff, and we're in the process of working those out.

While multiple discourses were present in the speech and actions of the faculty at Fernway, a multicultural discourse and a discourse of human relations predominated. These two discourses collided with other discourses to shape the meanings of two themes that were consistently mentioned by the Fernway faculty. These two themes were diversity and community. The faculty at Fernway drew on multiple discourses as they discussed these themes in relation to the children and families with whom they worked.

Constructing the Meanings of Diversity

At one level, diversity simply referred to the differences or variations between and among individuals and groups of individuals. However, its meaning was subtly nuanced as it was used within the different discourses that circumscribed Fernway school.

The discourse of human relations, a variant of the discourse of cultural democracy, emphasizes the humanness of all people as the commonalities and differences among individuals are recognized and accepted (Colangelo et al., 1985; Sleeter & Grant, 1994). Through this discourse, positive feelings are fostered among individuals as they interact socially with those with diverse backgrounds. These feelings will lead to a reduction in prejudice and an increase in racial tolerance.

Within the discourse of human relations, the role of the teacher is to help students accept themselves and one another through communication and interaction with those who are different from themselves. Teachers present affective activities that celebrate individual differences, which range from special talents and abilities to differences in language or cultural background. These activities show the commonalities and differences among all children, and they also increase the self-esteem of children from nondominant cultures (Sleeter & Grant, 1994).

The discourse of human relations is visible in the speech and language that is drawn upon by a number of the Fernway faculty as they discuss how they address issues of diversity in their classrooms. Ms. Knopp draws on this discourse as she describes her goals for her first graders:

> I would like them to be aware that we all need to respect each other as individuals. That we all learn at different rates. That we all eat different foods. That we are all very different but that's O.K. because we are all alike in many ways. We're all here to learn. We're all human beings. We are all living in the Fernway neighborhood and so forth. So I guess I see myself as wanting to let them know that initially you have to respect each other and we have to learn to get along. And then, there's so much out there and in here that we can learn. There's books to read and there's math, numbers, counting. There's nature, the Earth. There's a lot we can learn if we really make ourselves available to it.

Even before Ms. Knopp addresses the academic components of her first grade curriculum, she highlights the affective nature of her teaching. Using the discourse of human relations, she declares that one of her goals is to teach the children in her class to understand and respect each other as individuals who are different from one another. According to Ms. Knopp, individual differences, such as ability or cultural background, are personal characteristics.

In this context, addressing issues of diversity in the classroom means encouraging children to share their individual differences and pointing out how these differences make children unique and special. While Ms. Knopp emphasizes the differences among children, she quickly sweeps them under a carpet of sameness in order to promote feelings of unity and harmony in the classroom. In fact, this notion of unity and harmony is promoted throughout Fernway elementary.

At a staff meeting in February, Ms. Randall distributed a draft copy of a document she had written entitled "Share the Vision." Over the course of several months, Ms. Randall had conducted interviews with thirty staff members in order to identify "processes and behaviors that could make Fernway school an even better place in which to learn and work." Employing a discourse of human relations, Ms. Randall's document highlighted the need to respect diversity and the promotion of harmonious relationships. She wrote:

> If we exercise flexibility and respect, there is a greater chance that everyone will feel valued, held in high esteem, and inclined to help each other. As we become more diverse we need to improve our brainstorming skills, tolerating, maybe accepting (even welcoming) eclectic responses.

Ms. Randall emphasizes the need for respecting diversity so that everyone at Fernway will feel as if their feelings and ideas are validated. She also suggests some ways that faculty members can carry out this goal. She writes, "Positive communication and recognition needs to be increased. Send cards. Put up lots of artwork. Allow people to retain their individuality. We have an obligation to give praise to each other."

The ideas promoted in "Share the Vision" are already being instituted in the school. For example, there is a schoolwide program in place that focuses on "general anger management skills, assertiveness skills, and social skills." The school psychologist and the school social worker travel to individual classrooms to teach these interpersonal skills to children. The school psychologist explains:

> So we do a lot of teaching kids about feelings and getting in touch with their feelings and identifying how other people feel. So many people grow up and they don't know how to get along with others and they don't really know how to talk about their feelings, or they don't feel good about talking about their feelings, and we should be able to talk about it because humanity is really important. I think it was Einstein who said technology has surpassed humanity, and he's absolutely right. We are all so technological and we have these fancy computers and the Internet and all sorts of cellular phones and video games, but yet in terms of us getting along with each other and making this world a safer place and a happier place, we're not quite as far. We've got a ways to go. Our goal is to get kids to be able to feel better about themselves and to feel better about their relationships.

According to her, acknowledging and understanding one's own personal feelings and the ability to identify the feelings of others are the requirements for the harmonious interactions that Ms. Randall promotes. According to the discourse of human relations, teaching children social skills such as listening, responding, expressing feelings, and conflict management will help them develop more positive interactions and facilitate the building of relationships across gender, racial, and ethnic groups (Sleeter & Grant, 1994). The formation of cross-group relationships will reduce discrimination and prejudice.

The school social worker who shared the responsibilities with the school psychologist for teaching interpersonal skills to the children at Fernway gave an example of one of the activities that he presented to children in the fourth grade. He described a film which he had shown the children:

> The film showed a Hispanic grade-school-aged child who was going to get ice cream and had language problems and didn't understand what the clerk was saying. It was not a real good interaction because the clerk wasn't real patient with her. There were some kids her age behind her in line, and in the scenario they were laughing and kind of teasing her about [her language] and then they ran off. Later on in the video these two girls had a conflict over whether they could accept this Hispanic child or not. One girl wanted to because she was interested in this person. She felt that she was different and had something to offer, something to learn. And the other girl said, "She's different so I don't want to associate with her because it will bring me down."

After the children watched the film, the social worker involved them in a discussion in which he asked them to respond to specific questions such as, "How do you think the kids were feeling about what they were doing in this situation?" and "What do you think the little girl was feeling about what they were doing in this situation?" He then explained how the children had moved into more personal sharing about similar situations that they had experienced. In his words:

> So I asked if they had anything like that happen to them. And it was real neat. They were actually naming other kids in their classroom or in the school that were different, either by the color of their skin or the way they talked or where they were from. How they took the initiative to befriend these kids and get to know them and get to learn from them and share stuff. I was real impressed because it seemed to me that there were three or four good examples of kids doing that at least in the fourth grade classroom.

Although the discourse of human relations predominates throughout the above discussion, fragments of the discourse of cultural difference (Sleeter & Grant, 1994) are visible in his talk as well. Within the discourse of cultural difference, children who are members of nondominant cultures are viewed as being different.

The discourse of cultural difference can be heard in the words that the social worker uses as he constructs the language diversity of the Latina child in the film as a "problem," because it is not the language that is used by the dominant culture. He again appropriates the discourse of cultural difference as he constructs as different those children at Fernway whose skin color is not white, who have diverse language backgrounds, and who come from places other than the United States. The children who are labeled as "different" are those who are not members of the white middle class. At the same time children from the dominant culture are being told that they can learn much if they choose to befriend those "others." This activity attempts to make differences more appealing to children of the dominant culture so that they will be more likely to invite children from nondominant cultures into their lives. Harmony is promoted as white middle-class children are encouraged to interact with children from nondominant cultures because their "differences" make them interesting.

Through a discourse of human relations, addressing issues of diversity meant sharing individual differences. When this discourse became entwined with the discourse of cultural difference, difference came to be understood as those characteristics possessed by children who were not members of the white middle class.

While the discourse of human relations predominates at Fernway, a multicultural discourse also winds its way in and through the school. Issues of diversity are conceptualized much differently through a multicultural discourse.

Two of the faculty members at Fernway specifically drew on both a multicultural discourse and a discourse of human relations as they discussed how they addressed issues of diversity within their classrooms. Within these intermingled discourses, diversity referred to celebrating differences between and among cultural groups. Ms. Hatfield drew on these overlapping discourses as she discussed how she approached issues of diversity with the children and families in her classroom. Ms. Hatfield said:

> So I talked to [the parents] and told them initially that diversity is a real big interest of mine. You'll see your kids doing lots of work in social studies, science, all across the curriculum, just trying to teach them about different people and different ways of doing things. Just as an example, instead of having a holiday party I called all of these parents and let them know that we aren't celebrating the holidays. Instead, we had a big pot luck in the classroom. We had Hmong egg rolls and from India we had curry rice. The kids wore their native clothes. And parents came too.

Ms. Hatfield infuses information about diversity throughout the curriculum by providing children with information about different types of people and different ways of doing things. Within a multicultural discourse, schools are viewed as vehicles for celebrating and respecting cultural diversity and for providing children with the skills that they need to negotiate within multiple cultural contexts (Sleeter & Grant, 1994). Through this discourse, Ms. Hatfield celebrates the cultural differences among the children and families who are a part of the classroom community by inviting them to participate in a potluck meal. This activity invites children to share their cultural identities at the same time they are learning about the cultural identities of their peers.

Ms. Hatfield described other ways that she provided opportunities for the children in her classroom to learn about cultural differences. She often turned to community resources as a way to expose the children in her class to cultural diversity. For example, a field trip to the art museum on the campus of Midwestern exposed her children to artwork that was created by female and male artists from all over the world.

In addition to sharing community resources with the children, Ms. Hatfield incorporated multicultural children's literature into her classroom curriculum. As she stated, "I do read aloud every morning. Those types of books and those types of things are just naturally integrated into the whole ball of wax." She chose books that reflected diverse authorship as well as stories from other cultures.

Ms. Hatfield drew on a multicultural discourse and a discourse of human relations to explain how she addresses issues of diversity in her classroom. Calling upon a multicultural discourse, she incorporates multiple perspectives and viewpoints into her second grade curriculum. By exposing the children in her class to people, art, and literature that represent a variety of cultural groups, Ms. Hatfield promotes a vision of cultural pluralism. Children learn that their school community and the world community comprise many different cultural groups. Ms. Hatfield also drew upon the discourse of human relations by keeping the discussion at the level of celebrating difference rather than examining critically the historical injustices and the social inequalities that continue to exist between and among cultural groups in the local and global community.

Constructing the Meanings of Community

The second major theme that was woven through the conversations with Fernway staff was community. On a superficial level, community referred to a group of individuals who interacted socially with one another. However, just as the meaning of diversity shifted when it was used within a discourse of human relations and a multicultural discourse, the meaning of community also varied as it was used within these two discourses.

Drawing upon a discourse of human relations, Ms. Victoria Shaw, a first grade teacher, discussed her efforts to build community in the classroom. She said:

> You have to draw on the things that the kids relate to. . . . You try to talk about how we're different and how we're alike and you work on those differences and you work on how are we alike. We're all here for a reason. What is the reason we're all here? If we want someone to like us, what do we do? How do we behave? If we want to succeed, what are some of the things that we have to work on to succeed? So we're all working on the same thing, and we're all helping each other, and we're all trying to be to one another what we would like people to be to us–that's building community. And some years it's harder than others.

Through a discourse of human relations, Ms. Shaw describes a classroom community as a group of individuals who share the same physical space and who understand, respect, and accept one another. The sharing of individual differences and similarities bonds the class and helps them to establish common goals. For her, each individual child should be working towards the same communal goals. These shared classroom goals, coupled with the respectful attitudes that children hold towards one another, result in a community that is unified.

Ms. Shaw promoted community building through activities such as "Child of the Week." The children were each assigned a week in which they could share information about themselves which they believed made them special. Ms. Shaw said:

> Parents come in and bring pets or family albums or little sisters or brothers.... Now what has been unfortunate is some of the ESL children, their parents felt uncomfortable coming in. Last week we did have one of the ESL parents come in and she had an interpreter come in, and that was neat because the kids figured out that they asked the interpreter and then he asked her, and they all watched while the language difference was going on and they thought that was really cool. And what's great is that children are uninhibited at this age; they'll make comparisons like "I have a pet just like that" or "We lived in 11 different houses." We may be very different, where we're coming from, our backgrounds, but we do have things that are alike.

Through this process of sharing differences, children also make connections between and among their commonalities. Although Ms. Shaw works to build a community among her children, the notion does not stretch beyond the confines of the classroom. Ms. Shaw expresses regret that the ESL parents feel uncomfortable coming into the classroom, but she does not supply any alternative activities or ways that parents could be made to feel more comfortable. Instead, she places the responsibility on the parents to make themselves more comfortable in the classroom, citing with approval the example of a parent who brought her own interpreter.

Moreover, as Ms. Shaw speaks about the parents of the children in her classroom who were members of nondominant cultures, overtones of a discourse of deficiency emerge in her speech. Through the discourse of deficiency, children who are not white and not middle class are constructed as doing poorly in school due to their deficient home environments (Bernstein, 1961; Bloom, Davis, & Hess, 1965; Hunt, 1961, 1964). Through this discourse, children who come to school possessing beliefs, values, skills, and abilities that are inconsistent with those considered mainstream are seen as being culturally deficient. The parents of these children are seen as lacking in parenting skills and as being unable to care for their children materially or stimulate them intellectually.

Ms. Shaw draws on the discourse of deficiency as she discusses what the children in her classroom are unable to do: "They haven't got the skills of cutting and pasting. They haven't got the skills of what reading is about. They don't know that we're moving from left to right, and they don't have the sounds of the letters to put sounds together to make words." Ms. Shaw having arrived at the school with the change in student population, explains that such problems are new to her. In her words:

> There's a lot more lower income and a lot more poverty. There's a lot more divorce. There's a lot more high risk because either one parent has a problem with abuse or unemployment that's causing friction. There's this unequal balance of the families that have two professionals and the families that have one parent who isn't working. And so right there the importance of education in the family with employed parents who are professionals is different. It's kind of like a cycle that repeats itself. And the families that have been from low income the books were not nearly as important. Education was not particularly important. Reading to and languaging was not important rather than just plunking a child in front of the TV.... So that has made a big difference.

Through a discourse of deficiency, Ms. Shaw constructs the low-income children in her classroom as being academically disadvantaged due to their home lives. She contends that these children are having difficulty learning in her class because their parents do not value education or promote the right environment for learning. Through this discourse, the problems that low-income children experience in Ms. Shaw's class are constructed as being located within the child and/or within the family.

The discourse of deficiency also intermingles with the discourse of human relations in Ms. Knopp's discussion of her attempts to build a classroom community. For her, a classroom community is a place where "everybody is listened to and has their feelings validated." Ms. Knopp uses such strategies as cooperative grouping to encourage positive interactions among her students. However, these attempts at building community have proven to be unsuccessful with her current first grade class. In her words:

> This has been a real bummer of a year for me in terms of my class because they haven't gelled. You know sometimes they don't gel. I went from a class last year that really gelled to a class this year that, like I said, they're all marching to their own drummer. They have different agendas. And they are all for really good reasons. Most of them are the way they are because of home situations or parents who are in a custody battle. They're all feeling and acting the way they are acting because of what's happening around them.

Ms. Knopp blames the children for the failure of the class to coalesce as a community. From her perspective, the turmoil that children are experiencing in the home is carried to school with them. This turmoil lies within the child and prohibits the development of the unified and harmonious community that Ms. Knopp desires.

Ms. Knopp returns to the notion of the class community as she explains the frustration she is experiencing as a first grade teacher. Fragments of a discourse of difference intermingle with a discourse of deficiency as she tries to understand why she is feeling so unsuccessful this year:

> I've learned a lot with this group, and it makes me think that either this group is just a very different group and they're all having different agendas, or I have really fallen behind in how to teach or I've just lost my touch. It's either that as a teacher I'm failing or it's the class.

Through a discourse of cultural difference and a discourse of deficiency, Ms. Knopp struggles with the fact that teaching the children in her class is different this year. However, the discourse of human relations creeps into her conversation as she acknowledges the possibility that it may be something about her teaching, rather than the class itself, that is responsible for the lack of community. After 25 years of teaching, Ms. Knopp has gone back to school to get her masters degree. She then explains her masters project:

> So my master's paper is on kid watching so I can be more effective with the kinds of kids that we are getting now at Fernway. The ESLs and we talked about those. So that I can be a little bit more available to them and listen to them. Looking at them and reading their body language even if I don't understand their language.

Through the overlapping discourses of cultural difference and human relations, Ms. Knopp discloses that she has returned to school to learn how to communicate better with children who are non-English speakers. She draws on a discourse of human relations as she acknowledges that, through her masters project, she hopes to change the nature of the relationships that she is able to form with the children in her class. While she focuses on improving the relational aspects of her classroom, the curriculum remains unchanged. She continues to present all children with lessons and activities that reify Eurocentric ways of knowing. Through these overlapping discourses, Ms. Knopp works to assimilate children who are non-English speakers into the dominant culture.

In contrast to these discourses, a multicultural discourse extends the notion of community beyond the classroom and into the home. Ms. Hatfield draws upon this discourse as she discusses her attempts to build a community in her second grade classroom. She talks about the building of community as one way to establish stronger ties between and among students and parents, which she believes, in turn, allows for the needs of more students to be met within the classroom. Ms. Hatfield said:

> I feel that I've been able to make a real connection with the parents and they really feel a sense of community. That's what they keep saying over and over. We really feel that this class is a community. That even though some kids are really struggling they work well together, and they enjoy being together, and I really believe that's true.

From the first week of school, Ms. Hatfield attempted to build a classroom community across racial and economic lines. She organized a number of activities throughout the year for all of the children and families to attend. For example, during the first week of school she organized a swim party at the swim club to which her family belonged. She said it "was wonderful seeing parents from AFDC and parents who lived in $300,000 homes talking while their kids were in the pool." Describing how one of the white parents in the class had reacted to such community-building events, Ms. Hatfield said:

> I was just talking to a mom yesterday who was here, and she was saying that was one of the great things that she saw as a parent. She sees these parents, particularly African American parents, at [the grocery store] or something like that. It would be in the past where some of the kindergartners saw each other but they never spoke because they had never made a connection. And now when she sees all the parents, she knows them. . . . All the boys in the classroom came to her son's birthday party. In kindergarten and first grade it just never happened. It was basically white kids who came to the birthday party.

While Ms. Hatfield works to bring the families in her classroom together through social activities, she also actively works to involve parents in the academic aspects of schooling. She solicits parent volunteers to help in all areas of the classroom. Parental involvement ranges from putting up bulletin boards to guiding small-group or individual instruction. Through the involvement of parents in the daily workings of the classroom, the children work with and learn from adults who represent a variety of cultural groups. Ms. Hatfield initially invited parents to help shape her second grade curriculum, but, due to the mandated curriculum policy in effect at Fernway, she has encountered resistance from the other teachers. She explains:

> I really do try to follow the [mandated curriculum] because I have raised enough feathers here. I keep saying that I really have to choose my battles. In some cases I do deviate. . . . Before the year started, I had conferences with students, and I tried to get a feel for what the parents wanted their children to learn. What do kids want to know about? And it was really interesting I would say that 60 percent of the parents said the kids really loved dinosaurs. So that's the initial unit that I designed. . . . Again, everybody was doing something else, and I stuck out like a sore thumb.

Even though the unit on dinosaurs does not directly address issues of diversity, by specifically asking all of the parents to identify what they want their children to learn in school, Ms. Hatfield shapes a curriculum which represents the interests of all of the children in her class. It incorporates topics which represent the interests of students of nondominant cultures as well as those of the white middle class.

Ms. Hatfield conceives of community building as extending beyond the classroom, but she has built a community around the children within her classroom as well. Relationships are fostered among children and families that transcend racial and economic lines. The partnership that has been forged between home and school produces a classroom environment that is fundamental for the success of children from nondominant cultures (Grant, 1979).

The Fernway Community

In addition to working to build community among the children and families in her own classroom, Ms. Hatfield also works to build a community at Fernway school that is inclusive of all children. She advocates equal educational opportunities and the equal treatment of all of the children. Within a multicultural discourse, she attempts to build a community with other staff members at Fernway that is respectful of all of the children who attend the school and their families.

However, in order to work towards her vision of a school community, she is often placed in the position of working against the status quo. Questioning the entrenched power structure has led to numerous confrontations with her colleagues. These confrontations have arisen, in part, out of the tensions that exist between those teachers who advocate an assimilationist model and those who advocate a model of cultural pluralism.

Ms. Hatfield relates a story about seeing a fifth grade teacher grab an African American child and reprimand him in what she considered to be an inappropriate manner. In her words:

> I just happened to be walking by. [A fifth grade teacher] had this African American boy caught up in his chest like this, and she said, "Boy, I'm not going to tell you anymore!" And then they went along. I didn't say a word because it was not my business to step into that. But later on, I just had a chat with her. I said, "I saw you really having difficulty with that kid." And she went on to tell me what had happened. And I said, "You know, you used the word 'boy' to him and historically that has been a really negative word to use with black men and black boys." Just trying to give her some historical significance of what that word means to African American people. It was offensive to me personally. And I said, "You know," trying to tell her in a nice way of course, "if this mother had heard you refer to her son as 'boy,' I mean she would have been highly upset. Highly upset." After that I was vilified.

Ms. Hatfield works against the maintenance of the status quo at Fernway by calling attention to a racist practice enacted by a white fifth grade teacher. According to her, all such attempts are rejected, and she believes that she is perceived by the other teachers as not being a team player because she speaks out against practices that are harmful to African American children.

The majority of the faculty at Fernway draw on a discourse of human relations as they advocate a harmonious, unified, and tolerant school community.

Although this discourse promotes an understanding and an acceptance of difference, the underlying intention is to make all children alike by assimilating them into the dominant culture. The white middle-class power structure remains intact even as teachers such as Ms. Hatfield attempt to break the silence that surrounds the privileging of the dominant culture. This struggle to maintain the current structure of power is further evidenced in another story related by Ms. Hatfield about Fernway's annual Book Fair.

Each year, a major book publisher sends a number of books out to the public schools across the country and presents children with the opportunity to buy them. The school library receives a percentage of the profits from these sales, which can then be used towards purchasing books for the school. On the day of the Book Fair, hundreds of books are set out in the library, and children are encouraged to choose those books that they would like to purchase. They write down their choices on an order form and take it home that evening with directions to show their parents the list of books that they want to purchase. The parents are encouraged to come to school the following day and purchase the books for their children. According to Ms. Hatfield, who is the second grade chairperson, a small group of parents had written the following letter to express how painful it is for their children to participate in the Book Fair:

> Mrs. Hatfield, we don't think this is very fair that our kids are being taken down to the library for the Book Fair. They touch the books, they feel them, and they want them. But we can't afford these books. Could you just eliminate the touching of the books and just have the parents come that night and see the books for the first time, and our kids won't feel so badly when they can't afford these books.

Ms. Hatfield said, "To me [the letter] was very legitimate." She took the letter to the grade chair meeting the next week and shared it with the other teachers. According to Ms. Hatfield, they were incensed. The discussion centered on the fact that the Book Fair was an annual event that had taken place for many years at Fernway. They insisted that they were not going to change the way that the Book Fair was organized simply because it made a few people feel uncomfortable. According to Ms. Hatfield, one of the teachers at the meeting had gone so far as to say, "If these people don't like the school, why don't they just leave?"

Ms. Hatfield's story about the Book Fair illustrates another example of how much of the staff, through a discourse of human relations, views a harmonious and unified community as one in which the children and their families have been assimilated into the dominant culture. This story further illustrates the complexity of dealing with the underlying social problems that exist in schools and how difficult it is to work towards structural change. Although it seems that it would not have been difficult to honor the parents' request to organize the Book Fair in an alternative way, the idea was dismissed without even being given consideration.

There was no discussion of the possibility of doing something at the institutional level, such as seeking a grant or conducting a school-wide fundraiser that would allow all of the children at the school to purchase the books. Nor was there any discussion about reorganizing the Book Fair so that the children who could not afford the books would be spared the disappointment that their parents had written about.

The Genre of Fernway

The genre of Fernway school is comprised of a multiplicity of competing discourses. Fragments of many discourses are visible within the genre that surrounds Fernway, but the discourse of human relations and a multicultural discourse predominate. These discourses shape the meanings of diversity and community in very distinct ways and are responsible for much of the conflict among the staff.

More Change at Fernway

The competing discourses that were drawn upon by the faculty and staff at Fernway led to tensions that made life at the school difficult for everyone. During the month of April, these tensions reached their peak. A group of faculty members started an underground movement to remove Ms. Randall from the principalship. The actions surrounding the movement were effective. On May 2, Ms. Randall announced her resignation.

Prior to the announcement of her resignation, several of the teachers who had been at Fernway prior to Ms. Randall's arrival were looking for new positions. They no longer felt comfortable working in the environment at Fernway. Ms. Shaw was one of the teachers who announced that she would be transferring to another elementary school within the district.

By the end of May, the teachers had been introduced to their new principal, a white male who had been working within the district for many years. Ms. Hatfield feared she would "really have a difficult life" at Fernway, but she was unwilling to look elsewhere for a teaching position. She said, "I'm definitely staying, because like I told the social worker, 'They need me here.'"

It was in the midst of this uneasy situation that Ms. Gonzales assumed her first teaching position. Chapter 9 examines her first-grade classroom at Fernway Elementary. It focuses on Ms. Gonzales' practice and how she negotiates her first year of teaching in what she refers to as "a culture of turmoil."

CHAPTER NINE

Ms. Gonzales' First Grade

Juniper Gonzales, a twenty-six-year-old female, describes her ethnic background as "half Cuban, a quarter Polish, an eighth Irish and an eighth Austrian, of which the Austrian part is Jewish." Ms. Gonzales grew up in Claremont, Massachusetts, in a middle-class neighborhood which she described as a "small suburb of Boston." She attended public schools for twelve years and did her undergraduate work in anthropology at a well-respected university in Boston.

During college, Ms. Gonzales became heavily involved in children's theater. She enjoyed the time that she spent working with and performing for inner-city children and after graduation searched for a job in children's theater. At the time of her job search, such positions were not readily available. However, she was so committed to the idea of working with young children that she took a job as a recreation coordinator at the YMCA. In her words, "I wanted to work with kids and I kept looking for a job in child care. I took the job at the YMCA because it was the first one that I saw advertised."

After four months as the recreation coordinator, Ms. Gonzales was asked to assume the position of lead kindergarten teacher. At that time, having had no formal preparation in working with young children, Ms. Gonzales was required to take some education course work, which she thoroughly enjoyed. After three years at the YMCA, she knew that she wanted to go back to school to pursue a degree in teaching. She explained:

> I felt like I was at the end of the road in child care. I got the kids when the kids needed a down time rather than a structured time. I wanted to be the person that did the projects with them during the day and that taught them new things.

Ms. Gonzales was intrigued by the Equity Academy because of its emphasis on diversity and impressed with the speed in which she could complete it. She was admitted to the Equity Academy, completed the teacher education program in fifteen months, and was hired to teach at Fernway. Teaching at Fernway was not exactly what Ms. Gonzales had in mind when she made the decision to pursue a career in the field of education. She explained:

> [Teaching] is not what I thought it would be. I kind of idealized the world of teaching. I thought, "Oh, they have the kids when they are 100 percent focused. The kids are working all the time. They're getting things done all the time." It's different being in a school culture where you are dealing with other adults who have very specific ways of teaching and ideas about how things should be run. Some of that has to do with this particular school culture, I think, being a culture of turmoil.

Although negotiating personal and professional relationships with some of the Fernway faculty was difficult for Ms. Gonzales, this was not the case when it came to forming relationships with the children in her classroom. By her account, she and the children had formed a community in which everyone was involved. Ms. Gonzales said, "I feel like we are a community. I am connected to these kids and these kids are connected to each other."

The First Grade Classroom

There are 26 first graders in Ms. Gonzales' class. Demographically, the class consists of four African American children (three girls, one boy); three Southeast Asian children (one girl, two boys); one East Asian girl; three Latino children (two girls, one boy); and fifteen white children (seven boys, eight girls). Seven of the children attend the ESL Program. Ms. Gonzales describes the socioeconomic makeup of the class as "half middle- to upper-middle class and half on the lower socioeconomic end."

The physical interior of Ms. Gonzales' classroom can best be described as large, stimulating and teeming with activity. There hardly seems to be an open space on a shelf or countertop. Books, writing materials, math manipulatives, and science artifacts (e.g., rocks, magnifying glasses, a butterfly garden) are spread over the shelves and counters. Posters relating to topics of study are displayed along the walls that are not taken up by windows or blackboards. Colorful tissue paper cut-outs created by the children to celebrate Dia Los Muertos hang from a clothesline strung across the room. A writing center, math center, and "book nook" are positioned around the perimeter of the room. Ms. Gonzales' desk, nestled back in the far corner of the room, is piled high with books, papers, and projects. The only open area is the large floor space that is covered by a gray square of carpet. Large-and small-group discussions and activities take place here. Directly across from the rug are six child-sized tables and chairs. Children are seated around five of these tables. The sixth table holds more materials that children have used or will be using later in the day.

Number Towers

Ms. Gonzales and a small group of children are seated on the floor in a circle. "Today we're going to play a math game called Number Towers," announces Ms. Gonzales, smiling. "I would like you to keep the math partner today that you have been working with all week. Rick, will you be my partner for a moment so that you can help me demonstrate the math activity for today?" A huge smile spreads across Rick's face as he moves closer to Ms. Gonzales. As Rick situates himself, Ms. Gonzales passes out a bag of unifix cubes to each pair of children. She places a large plastic bag filled with small numbered tiles in front of Rick.

"For this activity we are going to be making towers," explains Ms. Gonzales. "Rick will pull out a number and read it to us. You will then work with your partner to build some towers to show that number. I want you to think about how we have been grouping things lately."

Rick puts his hand into the plastic bag and pulls out a tile on which the number 52 is written. Ms. Gonzales asks him to say the number and hold up the tile so that all of the children can see. After Rick announces, "52," Ms. Gonzales explains to the children that they can spread out around the room as they work to put their towers together. Ms. Gonzales circulates around the room observing children and asking questions about how they are thinking about their towers.

Alejandro and Ivan, who are partners, are having difficulty working together. When Alejandro attempts to add some cubes to the tower that Ivan is building, Ivan turns to him and yells, "Stop!" Alejandro, looking uncomfortable, begins squirming around on the carpet and playing with the cubes. Ivan yells over to Ms. Gonzales, "Ms. Gonzales, will you help me build the tower? There are a lot of cubes and Alejandro won't help." Ms. Gonzales walks over and replies, "That's why you and Alejandro are paired together. So that you can help one another." Ivan shrugs his shoulders and turns back to Alejandro. Ms. Gonzales talks them through the activity and encourages them to continue to work together.

After a few minutes, Ms. Gonzales calls the children back over to the carpet. She says, "I'm taking one deep breath and I would like all of us to be ready." As she takes a deep breath, most of the children take one with her. There is still some chattering among the children. Ms. Gonzales says, "I'm ready to start and I would like us all to cooperate. I would like us to go around the circle so that you and your partner can tell us what you did. Pete and Lynn, can you go first?" Lynn explains, "We built 5 towers of 10 and one tower of 2 so that we had tens and ones." "Can we go next?" asks Brittany. "Yes," answers Ms. Gonzales. "Well, we built 10 towers of 5 and had 2 left over." Ms. Gonzales says, "So you noticed that 5 was half of ten and divided those up and that there were two left over. That's an interesting way to look at the number 52. Did anyone else do that?"

"We didn't do that but our tower is the longest—it has all 52 cubes in one!" says

Samantha. "It is definitely the longest," replies Ms. Gonzales. "Trevor and Randi, how did you go about making 52?" "Well, we made 5 towers of 10 and put the extras back in the bag." "Hmm . . ." says Ms. Gonzales, "if you have five towers of 10, do you still have 52?" Trevor and Randi look at each other and shake their heads. "How many cubes did Rick tell us that we had to have?" asks Ms. Gonzales. Several children answer "52!" "So," asks Ms. Gonzales, "what can you do to make your towers equal 52?" "We can take those two back out of the bag! " says Trevor as he reaches in and pulls them out. He snaps them together and lays them next to the 5 towers of 10. "There," says Ms. Gonzales, "now do you have 52?" "Yes!" answer several of the children. Ms. Gonzales then turns her attention to Alejandro and Ivan. "That looks interesting. How did you decide to show the number 52?" Ivan explains that they wanted all of their towers to be equal so they built 4 towers of 13. "Ahh, you divided the number 4 into 52 and came up with 13 cubes in each tower. What made you think to do that?" Alejandro answers this time, "We just wanted all the numbers to be equal."

Ms. Gonzales smiles and says, "Now this is interesting. You have all made towers that show the number 52, and you have all made them in very different ways. Look around one more time to see all of the ways that you have made your towers. Since we have been working on tens and ones, I would like everyone to try to build their next set of towers to show tens and then a tower to show the ones—the extras. Lily, would you pick the next tile out of the bag for us?"

Lily chooses the number 21. Again, the class breaks into small groups, constructs their towers and shares what they have done in the large group. After they are finished sharing, Ms. Gonzales holds up some graph paper and asks the children, "Why do you think I would bring this paper over after what you have been doing?" Trevor says tentatively, "Maybe we're going to draw the towers." Ms. Gonzales says, "Yes, Trevor, you're right. How many squares do you think are in each row?" Ivan calls out "10." Just as Ms. Gonzales asks John, whose hand is raised, John answers, "10." Ms. Gonzales replies that he is right. She then asks Brittany how many squares she would color in to represent the number "21."

Brittany explains that she would color two long lines and one square. "You're absolutely right. For the next number that we pull out of the bag, we will make a tower and then color in the rows. I will be around to help if anyone gets stuck. Alejandro, will you please choose the next number?"

Building Community

The above vignette illustrates the themes of community and collaboration that Ms. Gonzales promotes through the pedagogy that she chooses to employ in this first grade classroom. Ms. Gonzales organizes the math activity so children can work collaboratively in pairs to build on the knowledge of the concept of number that each child brings to the partnership. Through the subsequent sharing of how children arranged the towers in the ways that they did, Ms. Gonzales acknowledges each child's understanding of this specific math concept as she affirms the fact that there are multiple ways to think about the number 52.

In the second phase of the activity, children are asked to think specifically about place value as Ms. Gonzales directs them to build their towers in rows of tens and ones. After the children have accomplished the tactile experience of building the towers, Ms. Gonzales moves them to a more abstract level of representation by asking them to color in the squares on the graph paper. Although this activity centers on basic skills in mathematics, it is indicative of the collaborative approach that she uses across subject areas.

Through such collaborative knowledge making, children are also involved in building community. For example, when Ivan calls on Ms. Gonzales to help him with his tower building, she redirects his attention back to Alejandro. She works with them for a few minutes to help them communicate their ideas to one another yet stands back and allows them to work out their own problems. At the same time Ms. Gonzales promotes collaboration between Alejandro and Ivan, she reinforces the notion that they are the knowers in this activity. In fact, it is the tower made by Alejandro and Ivan that, in the end, is the most complex.

Ms. Gonzales works to build a classroom community that fosters collaboration and minimizes competitiveness and individualism (Ladson-Billings, 1994). Through this multicultural discourse, children are encouraged to help and support one another academically as well as socially. By encouraging the building of community, Ms. Gonzales acknowledges the self-worth of each individual child within the group context.

For Ms. Gonzales, building community is an ongoing process—communities don't just happen, they need to be created and nurtured. She consciously structures activities and group situations that she knows will allow children to be successful. For example, Ms. Gonzales shared the thinking behind the way that she placed certain children together at the tables where they carried out much of their academic work:

> I made sure that Paul and Rick weren't together, and I know that's a relationship that I'm conscious of. I just place them in separate places almost immediately. There are a couple of groups of kids that I try to spread out, and, at the same time, I try to make sure that there's a couple of strong readers and not so strong readers at every table so that if we had to do a group activity there would be someone who would kind of take charge if there's any reading that needs to happen. Other people have more general community members, have different roles basically. Because if I had a table that were all not very good readers, they get really frustrated. So that's another sort of thing. I also try to make sure there are boys and girls spread out all over the place. Those are the basics.

Ms. Gonzales recognizes that not all of the children in her classroom have the same level of skills. She attempts to make certain that everyone has a role in the communities that are created around the tables by identifying the different strengths of children and placing them together so that they can learn from one another. She also organizes the table communities so that each is gender balanced, and, although she does not specifically mention taking racial and ethnic background into account, the groups are racially mixed.

Ms. Gonzales took pains to make sure that children with certain strengths sat together and also made it a point to separate particular children. For example, she noted that she did not place Paul and Rick, two white males, at the same table. She went on to explain that this was because they were always "acting out" by giggling, touching, poking, and talking continuously when they were together. Ms. Gonzales used the term "acting out" to describe situations in which "children are so into each other that they distract everyone else and themselves, which causes them not to be able to concentrate on the task at hand."

When children were acting out in the classroom in a way that interfered with their learning or others' learning, Ms. Gonzales first tried to redirect their actions with a look or a touch. If this method was unsuccessful, she turned to a more systematic method of classroom management, one which revolved around the use of what Ms. Gonzales referred to as the Beware Box. Ms. Gonzales explained:

> This is my Beware Box. It's like a warning system so that when I have given a verbal warning to someone already then the second time their name goes into the Beware Box and that says "Warning! You're about to lose a privilege." If their name would go up for the second time, if they would either get a second warning or they would continue doing the same thing, I would erase their name out of that box, and they would miss their recess. It's like a three strikes and you're out system.

Although Ms. Gonzales used the Beware Box frequently, no children ever got to the stage where they were required to miss their recess.

The concept of the Beware Box is a behavior management technique that stems from assertive discipline. Through assertive discipline techniques, teachers provide individual students with a clear response to their misbehavior. Ms. Gonzales did write the initials of individual children inside of the Beware Box. However, rather than simply using this as a strategy to single out individual children, she used the initials to signal to the class that they were now responsible for assisting that child by not providing an audience for her or his actions. For Ms. Gonzales acting out was something that occurred within a social context rather than simply being the disruptive actions of one individual. Within the classroom community, all of the children became responsible for helping one another to be socially successful. Consider the following scenario from fieldnotes:

> Ms. Gonzales is explaining an activity about teeth. Lynn begins talking with the others around her table. Ms. Gonzales stops her discussion and looks toward Lynn and the others at her table, "Lynn, I have already put your name on the board. Rick and Charlene, it is your job to make sure that Lynn doesn't talk anymore by not talking to her."

Through a multicultural discourse, Ms. Gonzales promotes social practices in the classroom that encourage members of the group to be responsible for one another (Ladson-Billings, 1994). When one member of the group is experiencing difficulty controlling his/her actions, Ms. Gonzales calls on the rest of the community to support and assist that child. Signaling to children in this way that they need to be aware of their actions and asking other children to participate in helping individuals redirect their actions are ways that Ms. Gonzales ensures that the social identities of individual children will not be constructed in a negative manner. When individual children take on negative social identities, they tend to become isolated and are set apart from the rest of the group. In Ms. Gonzales' classroom, nobody is excluded from the group as a result of acting out. All of the children are valued and respected as community members.

Next to the Beware Box, Ms. Gonzales has drawn a square on the chalkboard with the letters TT above it. This is what she refers to as Terrific Table points. Ms. Gonzales explains:

> A table will get Terrific Table points if they seem like they are really working well together. I usually don't focus on just one table; I try to focus on the whole class. If they are really focused on what they are doing, then every table will get one point.

Again, Ms. Gonzales turns to a behavior modification strategy as she attempts to build classroom community and collaboration. Children are rewarded for working together, and they celebrate their success through an art project or time on a given day when they get to play special games with one another.

Through a multicultural discourse, Ms. Gonzales promotes the notion of collaboration that was a central tenet throughout her teacher education program. This notion of collaboration was modeled at all levels at the Equity Academy. Recall that prospective teachers were placed in small cohort groups that were specifically arranged to promote teaching and learning as a collaborative venture. The cohorts were placed in the same setting over an extended period of time so that communities of teachers and learners could be formed.

The practice of building community is also carried out by some of the other teachers at Fernway. Through a multicultural discourse, teachers such as Ms. Hatfield create a classroom community that fosters collaboration between and among groups of individuals both academically and socially.

Collaborative Decision Making

Collaborative decision making is also a prominent aspect of Ms. Gonzales' pedagogy. A typical day in this first grade classroom begins with Ms. Gonzales greeting each child as she/he walks through the door. Children walk to their seats, take their chairs down from the tables, then assemble on the carpet for large-group time. The schedule, which changes daily, is posted on the blackboard.

By the time the school bell rings at 8:05 A. M. the children are all gathered on the carpet. Ms. Gonzales begins the day by taking attendance and the lunch count. After this task is completed, the class moves on to the calendar. Each day a different child is responsible for leading the rest of the class through these activities. The calendar activities, which have been adapted from *Math Their Way,* include posting the date, tallying the number of days that children have attended school, and counting them by fives and tens. As children carry out their calendar activities, Ms. Gonzales gets up from the carpet and allows the children to be responsible for this activity. When she returns to the group, she and the children discuss the schedule of the day.

The schedule looks similar to those that are posted throughout most elementary schools in the United States, but the way that Ms. Gonzales approaches this schedule allows children to make decisions about their learning. For example, during language arts, children read with Ms. Gonzales in what she refers to as "interest groups." These are mixed-ability groups of children whom Ms. Gonzales places together for the purpose of reading instruction. She introduces different selections of books to the children and presents them with the opportunity to choose which they want to read.

Ms. Gonzales also asks children to make decisions about the integrated thematic units that she develops. At the beginning of each unit, Ms. Gonzales asks children to brainstorm things that they want to learn about the new topic. She then integrates their questions and interests into the unit. Children are also asked to make decisions about how they want to carry out their work. For example, during a unit on volcanoes Ms. Gonzales uses learning centers for the first time. Children are asked to go to four different centers around the room and complete four activities pertaining to volcanoes. After completing the learning centers, Ms. Gonzales asks them if this is something they want to try again:

> "I just want to take a quick vote. How many of you liked the learning centers and think we should do them again?" Ms. Gonzales asks the children to put their thumbs up if they want to try learning centers again, their thumbs down if they don't want to do them again, and if they just thought it was OK to put their hand up flat in the air with no thumb up or down. Only two children have their thumbs down. Ms. Gonzales thanks the children and says, "It is important for me to know what you think. This way I know if we should do them again or not." (fieldnotes, 2/11/97)

Ms. Gonzales provides children with the power to make decisions concerning their own learning. Children learn from one another that they possess multiple viewpoints, perspectives, and interests and that they can respond to the learning environment in a variety of ways. Each child is assumed to be a capable and productive member of this learning community.

Ivan Authors an Identity

Ms. Gonzales is sitting in front of the classroom reading Arthur's Loose Tooth *to the children, who are seated at their tables. As Ms. Gonzales reads, Ivan, an African American male who is new to the class, begins to chew loudly on a piece of gum. Ms. Gonzales looks directly at Ivan and says, "Please go put that in the trash." Ivan looks around the room and continues to sit in his seat. Ms. Gonzales looks back at her book and resumes reading. Ivan begins to chew his gum loudly. Ms. Gonzales stops reading, looks at Ivan and says, "Ivan, this is the last time I'm going to ask you to please go throw that away." Ivan, sitting on his chair, begins to scoot it over to the wastebasket. He scoots past the table next to him, past the door, and, as he reaches the wastebasket, he scoots up close enough so that he can spit the gum right into the middle. While some of the children turn away from the story to look at Ivan, most of them keep their attention focused on Ms. Gonzales. Abby, who has been watching Ivan, backs up her chair and begins to scoot on her chair. Ms. Gonzales looks up from the book, looks directly at Abby, and says, "Abby." Abby, with a look of confusion, replies, "But . . ." as she points at Ivan. Ms. Gonzales shakes her head and Abby scoots her chair back into the table.*[1]

Ivan, watching the interaction between Ms. Gonzales and Abby, does a U-turn in his chair and scoots back towards his table. Ms. Gonzales continues to read as if nothing is happening. After she finishes the book, Ms. Gonzales explains to the children that they will be completing a packet of information on teeth. The packet consists of several activities relating to this topic. The first activity requires that children work together on some addition and subtraction problems. The children generate subtraction problems as they ask their peers about the number of teeth they have lost.

As the children move around the room to work together or to talk with one another about the number of teeth they have lost, Ivan plays with some strips of paper at his seat. Ms. Gonzales walks over to Ivan and explains that his work needs to be done. Ivan shouts, "No, I can't do this." Ms. Gonzales says, "Don't tell me that. I know you can do it." Ivan looks at Ms. Gonzales, gets out of his seat, and walks across the room. For the next ten minutes he walks around the room picking things up off of the shelves and looking at them.

Ms. Gonzales announces to the class that it is time for recess. She walks over to Ivan and explains to him that he needs to finish his paper before he goes out on the playground. Ms. Gonzales then walks to the door so that she can see out in the hallway as children are putting on their outdoor clothing. Ivan makes a run for the door. Ms. Gonzales catches him in her arms and redirects him back inside the classroom. He yells, "No!" and then runs across the room and throws his body into the chair. Several minutes elapse before Ms. Gonzales walks over to Ivan and asks what she can do to help him finish his work. Ivan shouts, "Let me go!" Ms. Gonzales replies, "I will let you go. After you finish your work. We don't always play games in here. We do a lot of work in first grade. Everything is not all fun and games. "Ivan yells again, "I want to go!" "As soon as you finish this page you can go out and play. I'm going to trust that you will get things done."

Ms. Gonzales stands up from where she was sitting next to Ivan and moves to the back of the room so that she can tidy things up. "I HATE YOU!" Ivan yells as he moves toward his seat. Ms. Gonzales continues organizing without responding to Ivan's words.

Creating Possibilities for Children

In addition to her emphasis on community, collaboration, and collaborative decision making, Ms. Gonzales consistently provides possibilities for all of the children in her care. The story of Ivan, an African American male who arrived at Fernway at the end of February, illustrates how Ms. Gonzales provides possibilities for specific children.

Ms. Gonzales' first grade classroom had run smoothly until Ivan's arrival. She and the children had created a community that was inclusive and comfortable for all. For the first three weeks after his arrival, Ivan resisted membership in the community and continually acted in the manner illustrated in the above vignette. During those three weeks, Ms. Gonzales refrained from reprimanding Ivan. Yet, as in the case of Abby in the above vignette, she would reprimand other children for imitating his actions. She also allowed Ivan to choose not to be a part of the group. He spent time wandering around the room, sitting off to the side of the group by himself, or even sitting on the bench that was located out in the hall. Ivan did not remove himself from the group at Ms. Gonzales' request but rather by his own choice.

Ms. Gonzales dealt with Ivan's actions by attempting to partner him with children with whom his strengths could be built upon and shared. For example, Ms. Gonzales asked Ivan and Charlie to cut the strands of yarn the children needed in order to make sun mobiles for a project on the solar system. She did so for a very specific reason. Charlie had difficulty carrying out activities that required him to use his fine motor skills. In fact, during the course of my visits to the classroom, he always asked those children who sat at his table to help him with activities that required him to cut. By asking Ivan and Charlie to work collaboratively on this activity, Ms. Gonzales placed Ivan in a position in which he was the expert in this area. Furthermore, by asking Ivan to cut the strings for the mobiles, Ms. Gonzales involved Ivan in an activity that allowed him to contribute to the entire group.

By April, the children were actively seeking Ivan out as an intellectual partner and as a playmate. Although Ivan most often chose to be with Charlie, a friendship that Ms. Gonzales actively fostered, he made other friends quickly.

Through a multicultural discourse, Ms. Gonzales "disrupted the notion that African American boys are social outcasts" (Ladson-Billings, 1994, p. 117) in multiple ways. First, Ms. Gonzales did not call attention to Ivan's actions in a way that would construct him as "the bad boy." She did reprimand him when he blatantly did things that were considered inappropriate in the classroom yet did not call undue attention to his actions. She would readily reprimand those children who imitated Ivan's actions yet oftentimes ignored the very actions that Ivan was performing for the students. Ms. Gonzales did reprimand those children whose positions were already established in the group for acting out on their own accord or imitating Ivan's actions. Ivan, on the other hand, was not yet a member of the community. He was in the process of authoring an identity (Bakhtin, 1986) in the context of Ms. Gonzales' first grade classroom community.

Ms. Gonzales constructed Ivan from the moment that he entered the classroom as a child who would succeed. When Ivan expressed to her that he couldn't do the expected academic work, she always insisted that he complete the work and assured him of her confidence that he could do so. She never doubted his intellectual capability nor did she allow Ivan to doubt himself.

Ms. Gonzales also arranged for Ivan to have positive experiences with other children outside of the classroom. For example, once a week Ivan and Charlie had lunch with Mr. Paterson, the social worker. Later, at Ivan's request, another first grader joined the "lunch bunch." It was a time during which the boys could be together, eat, and then play games in the company of Mr. Paterson. These relationships spilled over into the lives of the boys outside of school as Ivan was invited into their homes.

Ivan's family was referred to as being "a family in transition." They had recently moved from Chicago to Mayfield in order to find permanent housing. Ms. Gonzales never used Ivan's family situation as an excuse to lower her expectations for him academically or socially. In fact, Ms. Gonzales rarely discussed the family backgrounds of the children in her class. According to her:

> Family background matters because it gives you your life perspective, but it doesn't have to make you behave in a certain way. So, Ivan has a transitional life. It's really easy for him to fall into category XYZ, but he doesn't have to. There are always choices. My job is to show them those options.

As Ms. Gonzales' experience with Ivan illustrates, she works to provide all of the children in her classroom with the opportunity to make choices about how they want to construct their social identities, regardless of their family background, level of ability, race, class, gender, or socioeconomic status. Through a multicultural discourse, she provides all of the children with an equal chance to succeed in school (Sleeter & Grant, 1994, p. 175).

Take, for example, Dionne, an African American girl whose test scores, according to Ms. Gonzales, positioned her as "falling into the gray area between learning disabled and cognitively disabled." Because Dionne's scores fell in the middle of these two categories, she was not eligible to receive special education services. Although Ms. Gonzales' modified the assignments specifically for her, Dionne was required to complete the same lessons and activities as the rest of the class. Ms. Gonzales explained how she adapted spelling assignments for Dionne:

> I will adapt an assignment for a child. For example, in spelling you're supposed to write a sentence for each word, and Dionne doesn't write on her own yet. She's getting there. It's so exciting. I worked with her today, and she was identifying some letters. But anyway, for Dionne, I have Dionne dictate a sentence to an adult; they write it down, and she copies it. I still expect her to do the spelling sentences. I expect her to be able to manipulate the spelling words into language and to recognize that her sentences have meaning in the same way that I would do for the other students.

Rather than defining Dionne as deficient and expecting less of her in view of her "disabilities," Ms. Gonzales modifies the lessons and activities to accommodate Dionne's level of ability. Ms. Gonzales stresses that, even though she modifies the lesson for Dionne, she has the same expectations for her as she does for the rest of the children in the class.

Ms. Gonzales talked about her expectations for Charlie, who has difficulty using his fine motor skills, in a similar manner. Every time the class was assigned an activity that required him to use skills such as cutting he would say, "But I can't cut." Ms. Gonzales would either refer him to a child who could help him with the cutting, such as Ivan, or she would encourage him to "just do your best." Ms. Gonzales described Charlie in the following manner:

> Charlie is not very good at physical manipulation. He doesn't cut very well, he doesn't fold very well–things like that. But I would rather have him do it and practice doing that so that if there were an emergency he could cut himself out!

Even though Charlie has difficulty with his fine motor skills, Ms. Gonzales insists that he can successfully complete the same types of activities as the rest of the class. She often provides him with extra opportunities that allow him to practice his fine motor skills, such as the responsibility of cutting the strings of yarn with Ivan. These extra opportunities help Charlie to feel more confident in his use of these skills and provide him with practice that will allow him to become more competent.

Ms. Gonzales highlights and builds on the strengths of each child and helps them all become more competent in those areas in which they are not as skilled. She doesn't deny that there is diversity between and among children, but rather she structures learning situations that challenge and build on each child's ability to learn. Ms. Gonzales provides each child, despite her or his individual limitations, with the opportunity to find a place as a successful person in the classroom.

Addressing Issues of Diversity

Ms. Gonzales rarely addressed issues of race and class explicitly in her lessons and activities; however, she often introduced discussions about differences in gender, language diversity, and ethnicity through children's literature by reading aloud to the children at various times throughout the school day. The books that she chose to read during these informal times often addressed issues of diversity. For example, one of the chapter books that she read to the children was *Justin and the Best Biscuits in the World*. Although the topic of this book was African American cowboys in the United States, Ms. Gonzales used this book as an opportunity to address the issue of gender:

> "Women's work! I hate it!" Ms. Gonzales stops reading and says, "I bet some people other than women wash dishes and make beds. What do you think?" Several children begin to speak at once. Ms. Gonzales asks for children to raise their hands. She calls on Janice, who shares that her father puts the dishes in the dishwasher every night and that he also does the laundry. Charlie states that he thinks it is women's work because his mom does all of the housework. Other children share what happens in their homes. Ms. Gonzales explains that both she and her husband share the tasks at home. She then asks the children to think about how they share the responsibilities for keeping the classroom neat and describes how both boys and girls carry out the tasks of sweeping the floor, scrubbing the tables, and organizing things around the room. (fieldnotes, 2/11/97)

By acknowledging and questioning the sexist quote in the book, Ms. Gonzales disrupts stereotypical representations of women in this text. By asking the children to examine the sexist passage in the book, she also invites them to think more critically about the gendered roles that are traditionally upheld in U.S. society. She then asks the children to reflect on their own roles in the classroom, pointing out that gender is not a factor in terms of who does the sweeping, cleaning, and scrubbing in their first grade community.

In a later conversation, Ms. Gonzales commented on this discussion and her attempts to dispel the stereotypes that exist around issues of gender. She specifically mentioned Charlie as one of the children who had difficulty moving beyond gender stereotypes. Ms. Gonzales said:

Charlie has a lot of typically male/female gender lines, and he brings them up all of the time. So whenever he comes up with one of these comments I try to ask a follow-up question like, "I wonder, Charlie, could you do that too?" And then someone from the other side of the room would go, "Yeah, I do that all the time."

Ms. Gonzales acknowledges that gender discrimination exists. She attempts to disrupt examples of gender discrimination that she encounters in classroom resources or in the comments made by the children. By asking children to question stereotypical representations of gender, by orchestrating situations such as classroom cleanup in which children work across gender lines, and by confronting Charlie repeatedly with examples that run counter to his rigidly defined notions of gender, she creates cognitive dissonance in the children. As she does so, it becomes more difficult for them to maintain rigid categories and stereotypes.

Issues of gender and language diversity intersected in the classroom as children were introduced to such books as the Spanish version of *The Paper Bag Princess*. This story is a feminist fairy tale that both the boys and the girls enjoyed. On two separate occasions, I observed Alejandro, a Spanish speaker, reading the book and chuckling to himself. Ms. Gonzales, who speaks Spanish fluently, introduced Spanish to the class as she used it to speak with Alejandro and Grace, two Spanish-speaking students. She often gave directions in English first and then repeated them in Spanish. According to Ms. Gonzales, on one occasion she had read a story to the children in Spanish and then translated it into English. Since that time, the children had requested that Ms. Gonzales read to them in Spanish more often.

Through a discourse of human relations, Ms. Gonzales brings one of the three languages other than English spoken by the children in her class into the everyday happenings in the classroom. She does this through reading, providing children with books, and giving directions in both English and Spanish. By drawing on her bilingual ability in the classroom, Ms. Gonzales shows all children that multiple languages can be used to communicate knowledge in school. As a result, many of the children in the classroom have come to appreciate Spanish. By acknowledging and using Spanish with the whole class, she also validates the languages of the Hmong and Korean children and constructs language diversity as a positive attribute that children bring to the classroom. Ms. Gonzales also provides greater access to the curriculum for Grace and Alejandro by giving them directions in both English and their native language.

In addition to language diversity, ethnic diversity was woven throughout the classroom curriculum. Again, children's literature was often drawn upon to represent children and families from different ethnic backgrounds. During the month of April, for example, children were involved in an author study of the work of Vera B. Williams. Although Williams is white, she writes about children and families who are members of nondominant cultures. The class read six of Williams's books, including *A Chair for My Mama, Something Special for Me* and *Music, Music for Everyone*. These three books feature a young Latina named Rosa whose family experiences economic hardship. Through reading and discussing such stories, Ms. Gonzales presents the children in her class with representations of life experiences within an ethnic community. Further, she legitimizes the lives of the students and families who are members of nondominant cultures as she provides them with representations of their communities and experiences within the school curriculum.

Ms. Gonzales also brought ethnic diversity into the classroom through the celebration of holidays. She had made a conscious effort not to celebrate any of the December holidays because, as she explained, "I didn't feel like I as a teacher had enough information to fairly represent all children," but she did introduce the children to some others, including Dia Los Muertos (The Day of the Dead) and Chinese New Year. She explained that she had specifically chosen to celebrate Dia Los Muertos as a way to "balance out Halloween, which had become so commercial, and to try to show children where these types of holidays have come from."

Issues of Race and Class

During my visits to the classroom, the issue of race was directly addressed on only one occasion, and the issue of class was never explicitly discussed. However, Ms. Gonzales shared that, on two occasions, she had involved the first graders in discussions of social issues that surround issues of race. During a unit on the solar system, Ms. Gonzales had read the book *Follow the Drinking Gourd*, which generated a discussion around the topic of slavery. She also explained that she had addressed the topic of Thanksgiving with the children in her class through reading a number of books and viewing filmstrips. In her words:

> We read many different books and discussed what we thought each book was talking about. Then I asked them questions, "How do you think the Native Americans felt around that time? How do you think the Pilgrims felt? What do you think about it?"

Ms. Gonzales draws on overlapping discourses as she presents to the children in her classroom information representing multiple perspectives and viewpoints. Through a multicultural discourse, she discusses multiple perspectives of social issues. She draws on a discourse of human relations, however, as she centers the lesson around issues of difference and feelings rather than tying the discussion to the social issues that are prevalent in society today.

By choosing not to address issues of race and class in a more systematic manner, Ms. Gonzales declines to provide the children with a strong knowledge base that includes information about the historical contributions and cultural backgrounds of people of color. This is especially important for children of color because such information allows them to maintain their cultural identities while simultaneously transcending the negative effects of the dominant culture (Ladson-Billings, 1994, p. 17).

On only one occasion during my observations in the first grade did Ms. Gonzales directly address the issue of race with the children. This occurred when Abby, an African American child, brought it to her attention. The following excerpt from fieldnotes contextualizes the situation and captures Ms. Gonzales' response:

> The children are sharing art materials as they busily work on their pages for the class "Wizard of Oz" book. Ms. Gonzales circulates around the room helping children spell words and complimenting them on their work. Abby, who is African American, rushes over to Ms. Gonzales and says, "Tanya said, 'I don't like it when you're a black girl!'" Ms. Gonzales asks Abby to repeat what she has just said. Abby, near tears, repeats "Tanya said 'I don't like it when you are a black girl.'"
>
> Ms. Gonzales asks Tanya, who is white, if she could speak with her out in the hall. Ms. Gonzales and the two girls sit down on a bench just outside the classroom door. As she kneels in front of them, Ms. Gonzales says, "Girls, I'm hearing some pretty serious things being said here. Let's see if we can work this out." Ms. Gonzales turns first to Abby, "I want you to tell Tanya what you just told me."
>
> Abby, looking at Tanya, says, "I don't like it when you are a black girl." Ms. Gonzales then turns to Tanya and asks her if that is what was said. Tanya describes the story a bit differently. She explains that she had been sharing some markers with Abby and Eileen, who is also white. According to Tanya, she and Eileen had been talking, and they addressed Abby in their conversation. Abby had used a hand gesture which, among the African American community of children at Fernway, is referred to as "the ignore sign." Tanya, continuing with her version of the story, explained that she had made the sign back to Abby. At this point, Abby had said to Tanya, "You think you're a black girl and you're not!"
>
> Abby begins to cry. Ms. Gonzales says, "I'm not angry. I just want to know what happened. Was part of it a problem of sharing the markers?" Tanya says, "Yes, Abby can use the markers but Eileen can't, and we were arguing about that, and that's when Abby made the ignore sign." Ms. Gonzales then turns to Abby and asks her if she would like to say anything. Abby concurs with Tanya's version of the story. "Tanya and Eileen just kept talking and talking, and I just did the ignore sign. I wasn't trying to be mean. . . ."
>
> Tanya interrupts Abby, "That's when I said to Abby, 'I don't like it when you do a black girl ignore sign.'"
>
> "It sounds a bit like the game telephone that we play in here. Abby, it sounds like you thought Tanya said something else," says Ms. Gonzales. Abby nods her head in agreement.
>
> Ms. Gonzales says, "Let me tell you the part that worries me. Of course when we look at each other we notice that there are different colors of skin. When people start to be mean to each other because of their skin, that is not O.K. I don't ever want people to be mean to each other because we look different from one another. It sounds like a lot of this discussion had to deal with the sharing of the markers. Tanya, you may need to think about what it means when you decide to share your things with some people at your table

and not others." Tanya nods her head. Ms. Gonzales asks the girls if there is anything else that they would like to share with one another. The girls say, "No," and Ms. Gonzales asks them to shake hands with one another before going back into the classroom.

Ms. Gonzales takes Abby very seriously when she comes to her with the statement "I don't like you when you're a black girl" that Tanya made. Ms. Gonzales stops what she is doing at that moment and asks both Abby and Tanya to step out into the hall. She engages them in a discussion of the incident and allows each girl to share her version of the story. Ms. Gonzales acknowledges that people all have noticeably different skin colors, and she stresses that it is not appropriate for people to be mean to each other based on the color of their skin. She appropriates the discourse of human relations that surrounds Fernway as she describes skin color or race as a characteristic that makes people look different from one another. The underlying message that Ms. Gonzales sends to the girls in this situation is one of acknowledging and respecting cultural differences. Symbolically, Ms. Gonzales attempts to restore harmony and unity between the two girls as she asks them to shake hands before returning to the classroom.

By asking the two girls to leave the classroom to have this discussion Ms. Gonzales allowed a teachable moment to pass by for all of them. The entire class could have been involved in this discussion, which centered around issues of race. Rather than involving the class or at least including Eileen who was also a participant in the marker sharing, Ms. Gonzales took the issue out of the classroom. By removing the children from the classroom, Ms. Gonzales sent an implicit message that race is not something to be discussed.

Although Ms. Gonzales creates possibilities for all of the children within the classroom, she chooses not to provide them with the information and strategies that would allow them to construct possibilities for themselves once they move beyond the context of the classroom. Issues of race and class are avoided unless they are remarked upon by the children. When they are discussed, Ms. Gonzales addresses them at an affective level that deals solely with the feelings and emotions of the moment, removed from any political context. At the same moment Ms. Gonzales is teaching Abby and Tanya that they need to treat one another kindly and with respect no matter what their race, she is also teaching them to accept and work within the status quo. Teaching children to be kind to one another rather than acknowledging and explaining that racial discrimination, prejudice, and poverty exist because of the unequal power structure in society does not prepare children to work towards a just society that offers the same possibilities for all. This approach is consistent with the discourse of human relations rather than a multicultural, social reconstructionist discourse.

By choosing not to address issues of race and class in a critical fashion, Ms.

Gonzales allows children from the dominant culture to maintain their power and privilege in the classroom. As a first grader, Tanya demonstrates that she understands how this power operates as she names blackness and momentarily rejects Abby because of her race. Abby acknowledged the racial tensions that she felt, but Ms. Gonzales, through the discourse of human relations, dismissed them by covering the tensions with a blanket of kindness.

Although fragments of a multicultural discourse are evident in the speech and actions of Ms. Gonzales, she draws primarily from the discourse of human relations that permeates Fernway school as she addresses issues of diversity in the classroom. One possible explanation for Ms. Gonzales' appropriation of the discourse of human relations and her reluctance to help children think critically about issues of race and class is the conflict that she experiences around issues of personal identity in her own life.

Ms. Gonzales does not acknowledge an identity as a Latina. She describes herself as a "typical privileged upper-middle class white person with a European background." She further comments on her fair skin and blonde hair as she says:

> Visually no one looks at me and says, "Oh she's part of the nondominant culture." No one looks at me and thinks anything. I look like any citizen. Whereas Beverly Hatfield would walk down the street, and someone would look at her and say, "Oh, she's an African American."

Ms. Gonzales draws on a variant of the discourse of difference as she constructs members of nondominant cultures as being "different" from those who are members of the dominant culture. She situates herself as a member of the dominant culture, which allows her to draw on the power and the privilege which those who are white and middle class enjoy. Ms. Gonzales proclaims that her appearance is that of "any citizen" and constructs people of color as being "different." By situating herself in this way, she denies her own racial background. In her words, "I don't perceive myself as a minority. I think of myself as very much in the mainstream."

Even though Ms. Gonzales constructed herself as a privileged white woman, there were tensions that surrounded this construction. At times she drew on her racial status as a Latina to benefit her in material ways. For example, Ms. Gonzales was one of the "minority hires" at Fernway. Ms. Gonzales denied her Latina heritage on one hand, but on the other she used it when she felt that it could provide her with advantages. As she said, "It's like a hidden card in a way. It's a card that I use selectively."

The tensions that Ms. Gonzales lives with surrounding her own issues of identity may, in part, account for the fact that issues of race and class are seldom addressed in her classroom. By drawing on the discourse of human relations, one of the discourses that permeates the speech and actions of the faculty at Fernway, Ms. Gonzales is able to keep the few such discussions that she does engage in with the children focused on the differences and similarities among the children themselves. This discourse allows Ms. Gonzales to maintain her status as white and privileged while allowing the issues of power that surround whiteness to remain invisible through silence.

The Genre of Ms. Gonzales' Classroom

The genre that operates within Ms. Gonzales' classroom consists of two discourses, a multicultural discourse and a discourse of human relations. The multicultural discourse, and the notions about collaboration, reflection, and diversity that were carried within the multicultural discourse that permeated the Equity Academy can be detected in the genre that circumscribes Ms. Gonzales' classroom. However, there is no trace of the social reconstructionist discourse in which she was also immersed at the Equity Academy.

The reason Ms. Gonzales draws on the multicultural discourse to which she was introduced in the Equity Academy may be that a localized and particular version of this discourse is prominent at Fernway. Ms. Gonzales is able to retain elements of a multicultural discourse in her speech and actions because it is supported by some of the teachers with whom she works. As Ms. Gonzales attempts to become a member of the Fernway community, this discourse allows her to communicate with her colleagues in a meaningful way.

Ms. Gonzales draws on multiple teaching strategies within a multicultural discourse as she supports and nurtures the diverse personal characteristics of each of the children in her care. However, when forced to deal directly with teaching about issues of race, class, gender, ethnicity, and language diversity, Ms. Gonzales appropriates a discourse of human relations. The discourse of human relations, which is also supported by some of the faculty at Fernway, keeps the discussion of diversity at a level of difference and sameness rather than moving beyond to address the politics that surround these issues.

As I have suggested, one possible reason for Ms. Gonzales' appropriation of the discourse of human relations may be the personal conflict that she experiences in her own life over issues of race. The discourse of human relations allows her to discuss race at the level of difference while simultaneously silencing the power and privilege that are held by the dominant culture–a culture in which she is able to shift into and out of. This may also be part of the reason that Ms. Gonzales avoids appropriating a social reconstructionist discourse. Through a multicultural social reconstructionist discourse, issues of justice and equity are promoted in schools for the purpose of challenging the status quo and re-ordering society. Even though Ms. Gonzales does provide a structure for the children to succeed within the classroom, she fails to reinforce that structure with information and strategies that provide children with tools for dealing effectively with the racism, classism, and sexism that they will encounter over the course of their lives.

CHAPTER TEN

Implications for Early Childhood Educators

As I attempted to show throughout the book, the genres of early childhood education and multicultural education are comprised of a multiplicity of discourses that are socially, culturally, historically and politically defined. I attempted to identify a number of discourses that weave in and through one another to create each of these genres but acknowledge that it is impossible to create a "complete" or "finalized" genre, because discourses are dynamic and, therefore, always in flux.

During the course of the study, I found that I had great difficulty making distinctions between the discourses that comprised the genre of Fernway school. The nuances between the multicultural discourse and the discourse of human relations that were visible in the speech and actions of Ms. Gonzales and the Fernway faculty were particularly subtle. For example, there were moments when the discourse of human relations became entwined with a multicultural discourse and became a space of potential change. At other times, the discourse of human relations became limiting and authoritative, such as when it became entangled with the discourse of deficiency. Given the right conditions, any discourse can become authoritative.

Teacher Identities

Teachers communicate with one another in meaningful ways by drawing on the discourses that are available to them within a particular genre. As teachers piece together fragments of discourses, they take on the ideologies inherent in them. The continual negotiation and renegotiation of these ideological representations of the self is the process of shaping identities. According to Bakhtin, the discourses of others have a particularly profound influence over an individual's ideological becoming. In his words:

> The tendency to assimilate others' discourse takes on an even deeper and more basic significance in an individual's ideological becoming, in the most fundamental sense. Another's discourse performs here no longer as information, directions, rules, models and so forth–but strives rather to determine the very bases of our ideological interrelations with the world, the very basis of our behavior.... (Bakhtin, in Morris, 1994, p. 78)

This would suggest that the discourses in which the two first-year teachers, Ms. Nicholi and Ms. Gonzales, are immersed, in their teacher education programs as well as the elementary school settings, greatly influence them as they struggle to negotiate and renegotiate what it means to be a teacher. It is this appropriation of the discourses of others that shapes the attitudes, beliefs, values, and the types of student relationships that Ms. Nicholi and Ms. Gonzales are able to form as beginning teachers.

Ms. Nicholi is positioned within the discourse of normalization, and Ms. Gonzales is positioned at the intersection of the discourse of human relations and a multicultural discourse. In Ms. Nicholi's kindergarten classroom the discourse of normalization is comprised of variants of the discourse of child-centeredness and variants of the discourse of behaviorism. Although the ideologies embedded in both discourses are different, the notions of regulation and social control and the belief that development and the production of knowledge occur within individuals and outside of social structures or relations are carried within each (Burman, 1994). These fragments of ideologies live in the discourse of normalization that Ms. Nicholi draws from and authoritatively prescribe the standards to which all individuals must conform. She focuses attention on assimilation of all children to valued ways of being, defined by norms framed by the dominant cultural group.

The overlapping and competing discourse of human relations and a multicultural discourse define Ms. Gonzales' practice. The localized version of the discourse of human relations, when threaded with the discourse of deficiency or the discourse of difference privileges children of the white, middle class over those who are members of nondominant cultures. It reinforces existing relations and dictates conservative parameters for action. In contrast, the multicultural discourse works in opposition to the privilege that the discourse of human relations grants members of the dominant culture when entwined with assimilationist discourses. Unlike Ms. Nicholi, whose life-long experiences, race, and social class position her within a privileged discourse, Ms. Gonzales has lived within competing discourses. The tensions that she has experienced within her own life have provided her with an awareness that children and families from nondominant cultures are not treated equally in schools, and she draws upon a multicultural discourse to address these inequities. As these two discourses overlap, spaces that are pregnant with potential and possibilities are created. As James Gee (1996) contends, "bi-Discoursal people (people who have or are mastering two contesting or conflicting Discourses) are the ultimate sources of change" (p. 136). Positioned within two overlapping discourses, Ms. Gonzales is a site of change. This is evident in the way that she provides children (such as Ivan) with opportunities to shape positive social identities within a multicultural discourse.

The discourses that Ms. Nicholi and Ms. Gonzales draw upon as they author their teacher identities shape their pedagogy in very specific ways. More important, the instruction carried out by each teacher creates limitations and possibilities for the social identities of the children in their care.

Pedagogy and the Shaping of Student Identities

Ms. Nicholi's kindergarten can best be described as a teacher-directed, basic skills-oriented classroom. Drawing on the variant of the discourse of child-centeredness, Ms. Nicholi had initially encouraged the kindergartners in her classroom to become self-reliant and independent learners by providing them with opportunities to make choices regarding their learning. Children were encouraged to move freely around the classroom as they traveled among learning centers. The children had difficulty exhibiting "appropriate behaviors" in this type of classroom arrangement, so Ms. Nicholi deemed that they were "unready" to make decisions on their own. She further ascertained that the reason the children were having such difficulty controlling their behaviors was due to the chaotic home situations in which they lived.

Through a variant of the discourse of behaviorism, Ms. Nicholi attempted to provide the children with the controlled environment she believed was lacking at home. She externally regulated children through a system of punishments and rewards. Children were provided with knowledge and information as they duplicated projects, worksheets, and other types of lessons that Ms. Nicholi presented to them.

Individual children are recognized and acknowledged academically and socially through a system of rewards. In fact, helping children to be successful in the classroom is such a priority for Ms. Nicholi that, at the close of every school day, a "badge ceremony" is held so that three children can specifically be honored for their "appropriate behaviors." Yet many children were not able to meet the expectations for success in the kindergarten because the social identities that were imposed upon them placed their behaviors beyond the perimeter of what was considered "normal." This led to a reproduction of the hierarchy of deficits that existed at Woodlawn in the kindergarten classroom.

Within this discourse, African American males were positioned as being the most deficient in the classroom. Some of the African American males responded with anger and frustration to this positioning, which manifested itself in the form of angry outbursts in the classroom. Ms. Nicholi rooted these "abnormal" behaviors in the pathologic home lives of the children and considered them to be so far from the norm that she sought special education placements for them. The East Asian and Southeast Asian children were contradictorily positioned as a collective group of "foreigners" and as the "model minority" (Lee, 1996). As the "model minority," they exhibited "appropriate behaviors," yet they enacted their "foreignness" when the five Southeast Asian students spoke together in Hmong and interacted almost exclusively among themselves. Ms. Nicholi "did not even try to understand" these children and looked to the interventions of the ESL teacher and the classroom aid for providing the bulk of instruction to this group. Even the children who were members of the white, middle class did not live up to the ideal kindergartner who lived within the discourse of normalization. Several children had summer birthdays which positioned them as "young fives" and, therefore, developmentally behind their older peers. Although Ms. Nicholi believed that one of the "young fives" was cognitively advanced in relation to his peers, she perceived him as lacking in fine motor skills and recommended that he be retained. Ms. Nicholi's vision of the "ideal kindergartner" led her to call on a cadre of specialists in order to provide intervention for those children who were positioned outside of the norm. Through her subscription to the discourse of normalization, Ms. Nicholi defined these children as "not normal" and no longer considered them to be in her realm of responsibility as a classroom teacher.

The first grade classroom of Ms. Gonzales could best be described as a community. Through a multicultural discourse, Ms. Gonzales involves the children in her classroom in collaborative knowledge-making activities. Through collaboration, Ms. Gonzales minimizes competitiveness and individualism as she acknowledges the worth of each of the children in her care. Just as children are encouraged to support one another on an intellectual level, they are encouraged to be socially responsible for one another as well. When individual children are having difficulty controlling their actions, Ms. Gonzales calls on other members of the classroom community to support and assist that child.

Within a multicultural discourse Ms. Gonzales constructs each of her first graders as a child who will succeed socially and intellectually regardless of family background, race, gender, or socioeconomic status. She creates possibilities for all of the children within the context of her classroom as she acknowledges the diversity between and among individual children and structures challenging activities based on each child's abilities. Ms. Gonzales appropriates a discourse of human relations, however, when she addresses issues of race/ethnicity, gender, and language diversity. She keeps discussions of race at the level of difference rather than moving beyond to address the politics that surround this issue.

As first year teachers, both Ms. Nicholi and Ms. Gonzales worked hard to provide each of the children in their care with what they believed was the best education possible. They thoughtfully planned lessons and activities, put in countless hours at school, and were both held in high regard by their colleagues. Their teacher identities led to extremely different forms of pedagogy, which, in turn, shaped children's social identities in very specific ways. Even though the identities of these children will shift over time, each child's educational history will continue to shape her or his future both in and out of school.

Implications for Teacher Education

What implications does conceptualizing the nature of teacher thinking as a social endeavor rather than an individual enterprise have for early childhood teacher education? First and foremost, as teacher educators we need to be aware of the discourses that we use. We need to understand that the ways we choose to render our identities as teacher educators provide limits and possibilities for the prospective teachers with whom we work as well as the children who will inhabit their future classrooms. Once we are able to recognize the discourses that permeate our speech and actions, we can begin to make choices actively and responsibly about the pedagogy that we enact in our teacher education programs.

Second, prospective teachers must develop an awareness of the discourses through which they speak and act so that they, too, can make informed decisions about their teaching. Teacher education course work must include activities by which prospective teachers are explicitly taught how the genres of particular fields of education are socially, culturally, historically, and politically constructed. Teacher educators need to help prospective teachers identify and articulate the ideologies that are alive in discourses in order to make the concepts more concrete rather than keep the discussion at a level of abstraction.

One way to accomplish this is to provide prospective teachers with opportunities that allow them to compare how teachers, children, and families are positioned within particular discourses. For example, I have asked prospective teachers to read such personal accounts of classroom teaching as those written by Pat Conroy, Vivian Gussin Paley, Sylvia Ashton Warner, and Julia Weber Gordon with the objective of identifying the discourses through which the authors are thinking, speaking, and acting. Prospective teachers then analyze how specific discourses create opportunities or limit possibilities for children and families.

One semester in an early childhood course, I divided the students into groups and had each group read one of Paley's books. We then discussed the books in the order in which they were written, highlighting Paley's assumptions about children, including issues of development and diversity, and sharing examples from each book of teaching practices that she carried out in her classroom. Paley's work is particularly interesting because her thinking and subsequently her discourse, especially around issues of race, shifted over time. Paley writes about this shift in her thinking and reflects on how different her earlier classrooms might have looked had she conceptualized the children and the curriculum through her current discourse of race. If a class were strictly interested in the racial aspect of Paley's work, reading *White Teacher, Kwanzaa and Me,* and *The Girl with the Brown Crayon,* would provide ample material for analysis.

I have also found that adolescent fiction can be used as a vehicle to help prospective teachers unravel the complexities that surround the construction of their own identities as well as the identities of the children in their care. One text in particular, *Yolonda's Genius,* has proven to be extremely valuable because it invites the exploration of the different identities that have been fashioned by and for Andrew, an African American male, and the main character of the text (see Miller Marsh, in press). Throughout the book Andrew is positioned as a genius by his sister, as a slow learner by one of his teachers, and as "normal" by his mother. Using the themes and characters of the story, we examined our understandings of language acquisition and cognitive development through a variety of discourses.

Making the connections between the construction of Andrew as a first grader and the material consequences that result helped the prospective and practicing teachers understand that discourses are more than just language. The conversations we had about Andrew soon shifted into conversations about the children in their classrooms and field placements.

As teacher educators we also need to provide prospective teachers with opportunities to examine their own personal biographies in order to scrutinize how discourses of race, class, gender, religion, and sexuality have shaped and continue to shape their experiences and structure their world views. However, as Britzman (1991) contends, this biographical work cannot be reduced to the "nostalgia of the personal or the rhapsody of the unique" (p. 233). Rather, Britzman argues that teacher educators need to help prospective teachers contextualize their life histories by encouraging them to make connections between their biographies and social structures. Such biographical work provides opportunities for prospective teachers to examine consciously how particular ideologies have worked in their own lives to define their past, present, and future identities.

In order to help prospective teachers examine the discourses that have shaped and continue to shape their biographies in ways of which they may not even be aware, I ask them to create what Gee has termed *discourse maps* (1996, p. 190). Asking students to construct autobiographies in the form of a discourse map, working from the outside in rather than the inside out, encourages conceptualization of teacher thinking as social rather than individual. This backwards approach to autobiographical work allows them to trace the social origins of some of their thoughts and actions and simultaneously uncover some of the assumptions that have become embedded in their consciousness.

In the graduate level courses I teach, each student must craft a discourse map. The project consists of two distinct phases: a collective phase and a personal phase. During the collective phase, I divide students into groups who are roughly the same age. Each group is asked to list aspects of popular culture (such as television shows, movies, magazines, fashion, and music), educational influences (such as social studies textbooks, novels read, and projects or activities undertaken), and historical events that were significant to them. I then ask them to think about the societal messages, especially those in terms of race, class, gender, and sexuality that they received. I group the teachers generationally in hopes that they will be able to stimulate one another's memories. The information generated in small groups is then shared with the whole class.

During the second phase of the assignment, I ask prospective teachers to examine on a more personal level the information that has been generated collectively. I again ask them to think about the messages they received through the discourses that surrounded their religious beliefs, ethnicity, neighborhood, and immediate family, particularly in relation to issues of race, class, gender, and sexuality. They are encouraged to continue to talk with others, but their discourse maps should reflect the more personal messages they have received and continue to receive.

One of the most instructive aspects of this activity is the class's analysis of the ways in which male and female students construct their maps differently. Consistently the female maps highlight connections to others and the contradictory and constraining nature of the discourses in which they have been immersed over time while the male discourse maps highlight individuality and possibility. The construction of the maps and the subsequent sharing has led to some very sophisticated, and sometimes heated, discussions around the concept of discourse and the crafting of identities.

The types of activities mentioned here help teachers become aware of the discourses that they and others are using as they enact their teacher identities. They can begin to be cognizant of the power in discourse and make choices about the discourses in which they function.

Maintaining one's ability to work within two or more competing discourses is a process of constant examination and reflection. Teacher educators can provide opportunities for such reflection by providing early childhood educators with a forum for collaboratively sharing teaching stories (Abt-Perkins & Gomez, 1993) and experiences. Maintaining support groups for teacher education graduates once they leave the university and move into their first year of early childhood teaching is a difficult but vitally important task. I have experimented with meeting regularly with first-year teachers to share stories of the challenges and successes that they are facing in their respective schools. The group provided feedback for one another on issues of behavior management and curriculum development, but most of the talk was about how to survive in schools that emphasize high-stakes testing and rigid curriculum maps. The conversation centered around how to find a peer group in the elementary school context with whom they felt comfortable sharing ideas and talking freely about their daily struggles. They wanted a support group in their school that would function like the peer group that they had at the university. Such support for beginning teachers is crucial, and I continue to strategize with beginning and practicing teachers about how we might create such support systems within elementary schools.

Reflections

At any given time, multiple discourses compete for our allegiance and unless we are aware of our ability to choose to move between and among these discourses as we shape our social worlds, we cannot disrupt the power that they hold over us. Even an awareness of the power vested in discourse does not completely free us from drawing on those discourses that have at one time or another informed our ideological becoming. There are instances in this text where I draw on the discourse of child-centeredness and the discourse of Romanticism as I attempt to explain a finding or make an important point. These instances have been particularly jarring to me because they bring back memories of discourses that I, like Ms. Nicholi, appropriated as a kindergarten teacher. Although I find both of these discourses to be problematic for reasons that I hope to have made clear throughout the text, I am reminded that my ideological becoming is never finished and that my identities consist of the particular way that I have assimilated and combined the particular discourses available to me over the span of my life. This serves as a further illustration of how we, as social beings, are always enmeshed in multiple discourses and that we are all products of the social environments in which we live.

Notes

CHAPTER ONE

1. For another illustration of the use of authoritative discourses in education see Britzman (1991).

CHAPTER TWO

1. It is important to remember here that immigrant groups such as Jewish Americans, Italian Americans, and other Eastern European groups were considered "nonwhite" as well as African Americans, Asian Americans, Native Americans and Latino/Latinas (see, e.g., Alba, 1990).
2. Throughout the book I use racial and ethnic labels that are representative of each era. I do so in an attempt to be historically accurate as well as to provide yet another example of the fluidity of discourses.
3. There continues to be controversy over the class status of teachers at this time. While there is evidence that many women who entered the field of teaching were from middle class backgrounds large numbers of women from working class families entered the field of teaching as well (see, e.g., Apple, 1985; Hoffman, 1981). Once in the field however, teachers did attain middle class status. For the purposes of this book I will continue to refer to teachers as middle class.
4. At this time kindergarten teachers were referred to as kindergartners.

CHAPTER FIVE

1. It is important to note that the concept of "good" minority has become complicated by issues of immigration and refugee status (see, e.g., Ima and Rumbaut, 1995).

CHAPTER SIX

1. For a discussion of the various typologies of multicultural education, see Sleeter & Grant (1987).

CHAPTER NINE

1. While at first glance this could be interpreted as a gender issue, this type of interaction occurred between Ms. Gonzales and other children irrespective of race, class, or gender.

References

Abt-Perkins, D. & Gomez, M. L. (1993). A good place to begin—examining our personal perspectives. *Language Arts,* 70, 193–202.
Alba, R. (1990). *Ethnic identity: The transformation of white America.* New Haven: Yale University Press.
Anderson, J. D. (1988). *The education of blacks in the south, 1860–1935.* Chapel Hill: The University of North Carolina Press.
Apple, M. W. (1985). Teaching and "women's work": A comparative historical and ideological analysis. *Teachers College Record, 86*(3), 455–473.
Bakhtin, M. M. (1981). *The dialogic imagination: Four essays by M. M. Bakhtin.* Ed. Michael Holquist, trans. C. Emerson and M. Holquist. Austin: University of Texas Press.
Bakhtin, M. M. (1986). *Speech genres and other late essays.* Ed. Caryl Emerson and Michael Holquist, trans. V. W. Mcgee. Austin: University of Texas Press.
Banks, J. A. (1981). *Multiethnic education.* Washington, D.C.: National Education Association.
Banks, J. A. (1995). Multicultural education: Historical development, dimensions, and practice. In J. A. Banks & C. A. McGee Banks (Eds.), *Handbook of research on multicultural education.* New York: Macmillan.
Berk, L. E. & Winsler, A. (1995). *Scaffolding children's learning: Vygotsky and early childhood education.* Washington, D.C.: NAEYC.
Bernstein, B. (1961). Social class and linguistic development: A theory of social learning. In A. Halsey, J. Floud, & C. Anderson (Eds.), *Education, economy and society.* New York: Free.
Biklen, S. K. (1995). *School work: Gender and the cultural construction of teaching.* New York: Teachers College Press.
Bloch, M. (1987). Becoming scientific and professional: An historical perspective on the aims and effects of early childhood education. In T. Popkewitz (Ed.), *The formation of the school subjects.* New York: Falmer.
Bloch, M. (1992). Critical perspectives on the historical relationship between child development and early childhood education research. In S. Kessler and B. B. Swadener (Eds.), *Reconceptualizing the early childhood curriculum: Beginning the dialogue.* New York: Teachers College Press.
Bloom, B., Davis, A. & Hess, R. (1965). *Compensatory education for cultural deprivation.* New York: Holt, Rinehart, & Winston.
Bredekamp, S. (1990). Setting and maintaining professional standards. In B. Spodek & O. Saracho (Eds.), *Early childhood teacher preparation.* New York: Teachers College Press.

Bredekamp, S. (Ed.) (1987). *Developmentally appropriate practice in early childhood programs serving children from birth through age 8.* Washington, D.C.: NAEYC.
Bredekamp, S. & Copple, C. (Eds.). (1997). *Developmentally appropriate practice in early childhood programs* (Rev. ed.). Washington, D.C.: NAEYC.
Britzman, D. (1991). *Practice makes practice: A critical study of learning to teach.* New York: State University of New York Press.
Brooks, R. L. (1990). *Rethinking the American race problem.* Berkeley: University of California Press.
Burman, E. (1994). *Deconstructing developmental psychology.* New York: Routledge.
Carnahan, R. S. (1980). *The effects of teacher planning on classroom process.* (Tech. Rep. No. 541). Madison: Wisconsin R&D Center for Individualized Schooling.
Carter, K. (1990). Teachers' knowledge and learning to teach. In W. R. Houston (Ed.), *Handbook of research on teacher education.* New York: Macmillan.
Casey, K. (1993). *I answer with my life: Life histories of women teachers working for social change.* New York: Routledge.
Clandinin, D. J. & Connelly, F. M. (1987). Teachers' personal knowledge: What counts as "personal" in studies of the personal. *Journal of Curriculum Studies, 19* (6), 501–509.
Clark, C. & Peterson, P. (1986). Teachers' thought processes. In M. C. Wittrock (Ed.), *Handbook of research on teaching.* New York: Macmillan.
Cleverley, J. & Phillips, D. C. (1986). *Visions of childhood: Influential models from Locke to Spock.* New York: Teachers College.
Colangelo, N., Dustin, D., & Foxley, C. H. (1985). *Multicultural nonsexist education: A human relations approach* (2nd ed.). Dubuque: Kendall/Hunt.
Cole, S. G. (1945). Intercultural education. In F. Brown & J. Roucek (Eds.), *One America: The history, contributions, and present problems of our racial and national minorities.* Englewood Cliffs, N.J.: Prentice-Hall.
Connelly, F. M. & Clandinin, D. J. (1985). Personal practical knowledge and the modes of knowing: Relevance for teaching and learning. In E. Eisner (Ed.), *Learning and teaching the ways of knowing* (84th yearbook of the National Society for the Study of Education, Part II, pp. 174–198). Chicago: University of Chicago Press.
Cook, L. A. (1947). Intergroup education. *Review of Educational Research, 17,* 267–278.
Cunningham, C. E. & Osborn, D. K. (1979). A historical examination of blacks in early childhood education. *Young Children, 34* (3) 20–29.
Danielewicz, J. (2001). *Teaching selves: Identity, pedagogy, and teacher education.* New York: SUNY Press.
Dean, J. & Rosen, A. (1955). *A manual of intergroup relations.* Chicago: University of Chicago Press.
Delpit, L. (1995). *Other people's children.* New York: The New Press.
Derman-Sparks, L. (1989). *Anti-bias Curriculum: Tools for empowering young children.* Washington, D.C.: NAEYC.
Douglass, F. (1857). *Speech at Canandaigua, New York.* August 3, 1857.
DuBois, W. E. B. (1903). *Souls of black folk.* New York: Bantam.
DuBois, W. E. B. (1935). *Black reconstruction in America 1860–1880.* New York: Touchstone.
Elbaz, F. (1983). *Teacher thinking: A study of practical knowledge.* New York: Nichols.
Fairclough, N. L. (1989). *Language and power.* New York: Longman.
Finkelstein, B. (1988). The revolt against selfishness: Women and the dilemmas of professionalism in early childhood education. In B. Spodek, O. N. Saracho, & D. Peters (Eds.), *Professionalism and the early childhood practitioner.* New York: Teachers College Press.
Ford, N. (1973). *Black studies: Threat or challenge?* Port Washington, N.Y.: National University Publications.

Forester, L. (1982). Moving from ethnic studies to multicultural education. *The Urban Review, 14,* 121–126.
Frankenberg, R. (1994). *The social construction of whiteness: White women, race matters.* Minneapolis: University of Minnesota Press.
Gay, G. (1983a, February). Retrospects and prospects of multicultural education. *Momentum,* 4–8.
Gay, G. (1983b, April). Multiethnic education: Historical developments and future prospects. *Phi Delta Kappan,* 560–563.
Gee, J. P. (1996). *Social linguistics and literacies: Ideology in discourses.* London: Taylor & Francis.
Gollnick, D. & Chinn, P. (1986). *Multicultural education in a pluralistic society.* Columbus: Merrill.
Gomez, M. L. (in press). Learning to speak and teach in a new genre. *World Studies in Education.*
Gomez, M. L. & Abt-Perkins, D. (1995). Sharing stories of teaching for practice, analysis, and critique. *Education Research and Perspectives, 22* (2).
Grant, C. A. (Ed.) (1977). *Multicultural education: Commitments, issues, and applications.* Washington, D.C.: Association for Supervision and Curriculum Development.
Grant, C. A. (1978). Education that is multicultural: Isn't that what we mean? *Journal of Teacher Education, 29,* 45–48.
Grant, C. A. (1979). *Community participation in education.* Boston: Allyn & Bacon.
Graue, M. E. (1993). *Ready for what? Constructing meanings of readiness for kindergarten.* Albany: SUNY Press.
Graue, M. E., & Miller Marsh, M. (1996) Genre and practice: Shaping possibilities for children. *Early Childhood Research Quarterly, 11,* 219–242.
Grumet, M. (1988). *Bitter milk: Women and teaching.* Amherst: The University of Massachusetts Press.
Hall, G. S. (1901). The ideal school as based on child study. *The Forum, 32* (1).
Harding, V. (1970). Beyond chaos: Black history and the search for the new land. *Black Paper No. 2.* Atlanta, Georgia: Institute of the Black World.
Heath, S. (1983). *Ways with words.* Cambridge: Cambridge University Press.
Hemmings, A. & Metz, M. H. (1990). Real teaching: How high school teachers negotiate societal, local community, and student pressures when they define their work. In R. Page & L. Valli (Eds.), *Curriculum differentiation.* Albany: SUNY Press.
Hoffman, N. (1981). *Woman's "true" profession: Voices from the history of teaching.* New York: Feminist.
hooks, bell (1995). *Killing rage: Ending racism.* New York: Holt.
Hunt, J. M. (1961). *Intelligence and experience.* New York: Ronald.
Hunt, J. M. (1964). The psychological basis for using preschool enrichment as an antidote for cultural deprivation. *Merrill-Palmer Quarterly of Behavior and Development,* 10 (3).
Ima, K. & Rumbaut, R. G. (1995). Southeast Asian refugees in American schools: A comparison of fluent-English-proficient students. In D. T. Nakanishi & T. Y. Nishida (Eds.), *The Asian American Educational Experience* (pp. 404). New York: Routledge.
Kessler, S. & Swadener, E. B. (Eds.). (1992). *Reconceptualizing the early childhood curriculum: Beginning the dialogue.* New York: Teachers College Press.
King, J. E. (1991). Dysconscious racism: Ideology, identity, and the miseducation of teachers. *Journal of Negro Education, 60*(2), 133–146.
Kliebard, H. (1986). *The struggle for the American curriculum 1893–1958.* Boston: Routledge.
Kondo, D. (1990). *Crafting selves: Power, gender, and discourses of identity in a Japanese workplace.* Chicago: The University of Chicago Press.
Ladson-Billings, G. (1994). *The Dreamkeepers: Successful teachers of African American children.* San Francisco: Jossey-Bass.
Lareau, A. (1989). *Home advantage.* New York: Falmer.

Lee, S. J. (1996). *Unraveling the "model minority" stereotype: Listening to Asian American youth.* New York: Teachers College Press.

Lightfoot, S. L. (1978). *Worlds apart: Relationships between families and schools.* New York: Basic.

Lubeck, S. (1994). The politics of developmentally appropriate practice: Exploring issues of culture, class, and curriculum. In B. Mallory & R. New (Eds.), *Diversity & developmentally appropriate practices: Challenges for early childhood education.* New York: Teachers College Press.

Lubeck, S. (1996). Deconstructing "child development knowledge" and "teacher preparation." *Early Childhood Research Quarterly, 11,* 147–167.

Mallory, B. L. & New, R. S. (Eds.) (1994). *Diversity and developmentally appropriate practices: Challenges for early childhood education.* New York: Teachers College Press.

McCarthy, C. (1993). *After the canon: Knowledge and ideological representation in the multicultural discourse on curriculum reform.* In C. McCarthy & W. Crichlow (Eds.). New York: Routledge.

McCarthy, C. & Crichlow, W. (Eds.) (1993). *Race, identity, and representation in education.* New York: Routledge.

McCutcheon, G. (1980). How do elementary school teachers plan? The nature of planning and the influences of it. *Elementary School Journal, 81,* 4–23.

McLaren, P. (1989). *Life in Schools.* New York: Longman.

McLaren, P. (1994). White terror and oppositional agency: Towards a critical multiculturalism. In D. Goldberg (Ed.), *Multiculturalism: A critical reader.* Cambridge: Blackwell.

Metz, M. H. (1989). Real school: A universal drama amid disparate experience. In Mitchell & Goertz (Eds.), *Education politics for the new century: The twentieth anniversary yearbook of the Politics of Education Association.* New York: Falmer.

Miller Marsh, M. (in press). The shaping of Ms. Nicholi: The discursive fashioning of teacher identities. *International Journal of Qualitative Studies in Education.*

Mohraz, J. J. (1979). *The separate problem: Case studies of Black education in the North, 1900–1930.* Westport, Conn.: Greenwood.

Morine-Dershimer, G. (1979). *Teacher plan and classroom reality: The South Bay study: Part 4* (Research Series No. 60). East Lansing: Michigan State University, Institute for Research on Teaching.

Morris, P. (Ed.). (1994). *The Bakhtin reader: Selected writings of Bakhtin, Medvedev, Volosinov.* London: Arnold.

Munby, H. (1982). The place of teacher beliefs in research on teacher thinking and decision making, and an alternative methodology. *Instructional Science, 11,* 201–225.

Nicholson, L. & Seidman, S. (Eds.). (1995). *Social postmodernism, beyond identity politics.* New York: Cambridge University Press.

Olneck, M. R. (1990). The recurring dream: Symbolism and ideology in intercultural and multicultural education. *American Journal of Education, 98* (2), 147–175.

Peterson, P. L., Marx, R. W., & Clark, C. M. (1978). Teacher planning, teacher behavior, and student achievement. *American Educational Research Journal, 15,* 417–432.

Popkewitz, T. (1993). *A political sociology of educational reform: Power/knowledge in teaching, teacher education, and research.* New York: Teachers College Press.

Quam, S. (1988). *First kindergarten in the United States.* Watertown, Wisconsin: Watertown Historical Society.

Rethinking Schools: An Urban Education Journal. Milwaukee, Wisconsin.

Rothman, S. (1978). *Woman's proper place: A history of changing ideals and practices, 1870 to the present.* New York: Basic.

Shapiro, M. J. (1988). *The politics of representation: Writing practices in biography, photography, and policy analysis.* Madison, Wisconsin: The University of Wisconsin Press.

Shavelson, R. & Stern, P. (1981). Research on teachers' pedagogical thoughts, judgments, decisions and behavior. *Review of Educational Research, 51* (4), 455–498.

Sleeter, C. E. (Ed.) (1991). *Empowerment through multicultural education.* Albany: SUNY University Press.

Sleeter, C. E. & Grant, C. A. (1987). An analysis of multicultural education in the United States. *Harvard Educational Review, 7,* 421–444.

Sleeter, C. E. & Grant, C. A. (1994). *Making choices for multicultural education: Five approaches to race, class and gender.* Englewood Cliffs, N.J.: Prentice-Hall.

Spodek, B. (1988). Implicit theories of early childhood teachers: Foundations for professional behavior. In B. Spodek, O. N. Saracho, & D. L. Peters (Eds.), *Professionalism and the early childhood practitioner.* New York: Teachers College Press.

Takaki, R. (1993). *A different mirror: A history of multicultural America.* Boston: Little.

Tharp, R. G. & Gallimore, R. (1988). *Rousing minds to life.* New York: Cambridge University Press.

Vickery, W. & Cole, S. (1943). *Intercultural education in American schools: Proposed objectives and methods.* New York: Harper.

Villegas, A. M. (1988). School failure and cultural mismatch: Another view. *The Urban Review, 204,* 253–265.

Volosinov, V. (1973). *Marxism and the philosophy of language.* New York: Seminar.

Vygotsky, L. S. (1978). *Mind in society: The development of higher psychological processes,* Eds. M. Cole, V. John-Steiner, S. Scribner, and E. Soubermen. Cambridge: Harvard University Press.

Watertown Historical Society. (1988). *Froebel's gifts.* Watertown, Wisconsin.

Watson, J. B. (1925). *Behaviorism.* New York: W.W. Norton.

Watts, W. A. (1984). Attitude change: Theories and methods. In R. L. Jones (Ed.), *Attitudes and attitude change in special education: Theory and practice* (pp. 41–69)., VA: Council for Exceptional Children.

Weber, E. (1984). *Ideas influencing early childhood education: A theoretical analysis.* New York: Teachers College Press.

White, A. O. (1973). The Black leadership class and education in ante-bellum Boston. *Journal of Negro Education, 42,* 505–515.

Wickersham, J. P. (1969). *A history of education in Pennsylvania.* New York: Arno and The New York Times.

Woodson, C. (1933). *The mis-education of the Negro.* Washington, D.C.: Associated.

Zahorik, J. A. (1970). The effects of planning on teaching. *Elementary School Journal, 71,* 143–151.

Zeichner, K. (1994). Personal renewal and social construction through teacher research. In S. Hollingsworth & H. Sockett (Eds.). *Teacher Research and educational reform: Ninety-third yearbook of the National Society for the Study of Education* (pp. 66–84). Chicago: University of Chicago Press.

Index

Page numbers in *italics* refer to tables or illustrations.

A Chair for My Mama (Williams), 144
Abt-Perkins, D., 156
action research, 107
Advanced Opportunity Fellowships, 110
An Essay on the Education of Female Teachers (Beecher), 19
Anti-bias Curriculum: Tools for Empowering Young Children (Derman-Sparks), 38
Apple, M., 19
appropriate behaviors, 54
assertive discipline, 135
authoring an identity, 140
authoritative discourses, 8–9

Bakhtin, M. M., 5, 6, 8, 140, 150
Banks, J. A., 87, 88, 90, 91, 94
Beecher, C., 19, 45
behavior modification, 24
behaviorism, 23
Berk, L. E., 26
Bernstein, B., 25, 123
Biklen, S. K., 20
black power, 92
Bloch, M., 16, 17, 18, 22
Bloom, B., 25, 123
Blume, J., 32
Boetcher, D., 38
Braun, L., 33
Bredekamp, S., 15, 26
Britzman, D., 3, 155

Brooks, R. L., 88
Brown v. Board of Education, 92
Bullough, R., 100
Bureau for Intercultural Education, 91
Burman, E., 7, 24, 33, 151

Campus Nursery School, 28
Carter, K., 3, 5
Casey, K., 3
child care, 16
 in the early 1800s, 17
child-centeredness, 24, 38
 and the Civil Rights Movement, 25
 discourses, *43*
child development philosophy, 26
Chinn, P., 95
Civil Rights Movement, 87, 93, 96
Christianity, 16
Clandinin, D. J., 3, 4
Clark, C., 3
classroom knowledge, 5
Cleverley, J., 17
Colangelo, N., 118
Cole, S., 90, 91
collaborative knowledge making, 134
Connelly, F. M., 3, 4
Conroy, P., 154
Cook, L. A., 91
Copple, C., 26
Counts, G. S., 31

168   The Social Fashioning of Teacher Identities

Crichlow, W., 104
critical sociocultural discourse, 33, 34, 37, *43*
cultural democracy, 91
cultural evolution, 20
culturally relevant pedagogy, 80
Cunningham, C. E., 16, 18

Danielewitz, J., 3
Darwin, C., 20
Davis, A., 25, 123
day nurseries, 19
Delpit, L., 71, 79
Department of Public Instruction (Ohio), 28
Derman-Sparks, L., 38, 62
developmental progression, 32
developmentalists, 20, 21
Developmentally Appropriate Practice in Early Childhood Programs (Bredekamp and Copple), 26
direct instructional strategies, 24
discourse
  maps, 155
  of behaviorism, 71, 83, 151
  of child-centeredness, 31, 60, 70, 79, 83, 151
  and the meaning of development, 75
  of classroom practice, 4
  of critical multiculturalism, 97
  of cultural difference, 120
  of deficiency, 123–24
  of domesticity, 57
  of human relations, 117, 118, 121, 123
  of normalization, 54, 55, 63, 83, 151
  of social reconstruction, 31
discourses
  authoritative, 8–9
  definition of, 9
  internally persuasive, 8, 9
  of anti-colonialism, 93
  of black and ethnic power, 92–94
  of cultural competence, 96
  of cultural democracy, 91
  of cultural emancipation, 96–97
  of cultural understanding, 96
  of developmentally appropriate practices (DAP), 25–27
    guidelines for, 26
    Piagetian theory and, 27
  of harmony, understanding and acceptance, 90–92
  of multicultural education, 94–97, 101
  of race cognizance, 93
  of race consciousness and race pride, 87–90, 92
  of social reconstructionism, 101
disempowerment, 79
diversity
  definition of, 35
domestic and manual training courses, 21
Douglass, F., 88
DuBois, W. E. B., 87, 88, 89
dysconscious racism, 115

early childhood education, 2
  and authoritative discourses of religion and science, 15
  and behaviorism, 23
  charting the genre of, 15
  and child-centered programs, 24
  child development philosophy in, 26
  implications for, 150
  in the colonial era, 16–17
    description of teachers, 16–17
  in the early 1800s, 17
  for girls, 16
  and literacy, 37
  multiplicity of discourses, 150
  shaping of student identities, 152
  and standardized tests, 22
  teacher identities and, 150–52
  teaching basic skills in, 25
Early Education Program (EEP), 27, 29, 66, 83
  constructing meanings of collaboration, 41–42
  constructing meanings of development, 31–34
  constructing meanings of diversity, 34–38
  constructing meanings of thoughtful teaching, 38–41
  description of program, 29–31
    field placements, 29
  genre of, 42–44
  program themes, *43*
Elbaz, F., 4
emancipation, 24
English as a Second Language (ESL), 80, 113
Equity Academy, 11, 97, 98, 99–108, 148
  constructing the meaning of change at, 102–4
  constructing the meaning of collaboration at, 107

constructing the meaning of diversity at, 104–5
constructing the meaning of reflective teaching at, 106–7
courseload at, *101*
discourses of multiculturalism used at, 101
discourses of reconstructionism used at, 101
emphasis of, 98
genre of, 108–9
high attrition rate at, 109
integrated curriculum at, 100
and multicultural cohort groups, 109
purpose of, 98
structure of program, 99–100
student demographics, 110
use of action research at, 106
use of literacy biographies at, 105

facilitating learning, 32
Fairclough, N. L., 7
Family Socioeconomic Problem-Solving Project, 35
Fernway Elementary School, 11, 111
 affects of subsidized housing, 113
 Book Fair at, 128–29
 conflict among faculty, 117
 constructing the meanings of community at, 122–27
 constructing the meanings of diversity at, 118–22
 description of faculty at, 116
 description of Fernway community, 127–29
 description of school, 112
 description of student body, 112–13
 genre of, 129
 mobility of students, 114
 proof of heterogeneity chart usage at, 116
 racism at, 115, 127
 segregation at, 115–16
 use of discourse of human relations at, 117, 118
 use of multicultural discourse at, 117
 and white flight, 113
Finkelstein, B., 22
Follow the Drinking Gourd, 144
Ford, N., 93
Forester, L., 94
Frankenberg, R., 16, 88, 92, 93
Freedom Schools, 20

Freud, S., 23
Froebel, F., 17, 18, 24, 45

Gallimore, R., 26
Gay, G., 93, 95
Gee, J., 7, 151, 155
General Assembly of Philadelphia, 16
Gesell, A., 24
"gift of time," 75
Girl with the Brown Crayon, The (Paley), 155
Gitlin, A., 100
Goddard, H. H., 21
Gollnick, D., 95
Gomez, M. L., 3, 156
Gonzales, J., 10, 11, 97, 111, 129, 151, 152, 153
 admission to Equity Academy, 120–31
 background of, 130
 Beware Box, 135, 136
 building community in the classroom, 133–36
 collaborative decision making, 137–38
 creating possibilities for children, 139–42
 daytime schedule in the classroom, 137
 description of first grade classroom, 131
 genre of classroom, 148–49
 issues of diversity, 142–44
 issues of gender discrimination, 143
 issues of race and class in the classroom, 144–48
 notion of collaboration, 136
 Terrific Table, 136
 use of assertive discipline, 135
 use of discourse of human relations, 147
 use of multicultural discourse, 147
 use of Spanish in the classroom, 143
 varying student skill levels, 135
Gordon, J. W., 154
Grant, C. A., 87, 95, 101, 118, 120, 121, 127, 141
Graue, M. E., 5, 75
Greenspan, E., 49, 53, 62
Grimke, B., 58
Grumet, M., 19

Hall, G. S., 20
Harding, V., 92, 93
Harris, W., 22
Hatfield, B., 116, 117, 121, 126, 127, 128, 129
 use of multicultural children's literature in class, 122

Head Start, 25, 54
Heath, S., 36
Hebron House, 103
Hess, R., 25, 123
Hilltop Elementary School, 99
History of the Negro Race in America (Williams), 89
Hoffman, N., 16, 17, 19, 20
hooks, b., 115
human relations, 92
Hunt, J. M., 25, 123

identities, 10
ideology, 9
indigenous literacies, 105
infant school, 17
Institute of the Black World, 92
integrated curriculum, 100
intercultural education, 91, 92
Intercultural Education Movement, 87
interindividual territory, 5, 8
internally persuasive discourses, 8, 9
intellectual history framework, 40
issues of representation, 96

Jackson, E., 99, 100, 101, 104, 109, 110
Johnson, L. B., 25
Justin and the Best Biscuits in the World, 142

Kessler, S., 26
kindergarten magnet program (Woodlawn Elementary School), 51, 55
 curriculum at, 58, 59
 report card, 58–61
kindergartens
 early history of, 18
 and teachers, 22
 as professionals, 22
King, J. E., 115
Kliebard, H., 20, 22, 31
Knopp, K., 116, 117, 118, 124, 125
Kondo, D., 8
Kwanza and Me (Paley), 155

Ladies' Magazine, 18
Ladson-Billings, G., 71, 80, 134, 136, 140, 145
Landmere Elementary School, 99
language, 6–7, 26

Lee, S. J., 80, 81, 153
Lightfoot, S. L., 16
literacy, 37
literacy autobiographies, 105
Locke, J., 23
Lubeck, S., 26

Mallory, B. L., 26
Marx, R. W., 3
McCarthy, C., 96, 104
McCutcheon, G., 4
McLaren, P., 31, 96
meaning of development, 75
measuring development, 32
Meyer, K., 98, 99, 106
Midwestern University, 27, 28, 66, 81, 83, 107, 122
 Department of Curriculum and Instruction, 98
Miller Marsh, M., 3, 5
Mis-education of the Negro, The (Woodson), 89
"model minority," 80, 153
Mohraz, J. J., 20
Morine-Dershimer, G., 4
Morris, P., 151
multicultural cohort groups, 109
multicultural discourse, 117, 121
multicultural education, 11
 conservative discourses of, 96
 critics of, 95–96
 discourses of, 94–97
 genre of, 87
 history of, 87–88
 at Woodlawn Elementary School, 61–62
multicultural literature, 1
Multicultural Night (Woodlawn Elementary School), 62
multiethnic education, 94
 Also see multicultural education
Munby, H., 4
Music, Music for Everyone (Williams), 144

National Association for the Education of Young Children (NAEYC), 15, 26
National Teacher Corps, 98
New, R. S., 26
New York State Charities Aid Association, 19
Negro History Bulletin, 90
Negro History Week, 90, 92

Nicholi, A., 10, 11, 27, 46, 64, 151, 152, 153
  background of, 65
  description of daily classroom schedule, 69–70
  description of her kindergarten classroom, 66–68
    as a teacher directed program, 68
  disempowerment of students in her classroom, 79
  expectation for "appropriate behavior," 72
  expectation for conformity, 72
  genre of, 83–84
  on Head Start program, 54
  hiring at Woodlawn Elementary School, 66
  imposing identities upon her students, 78–81
  lowering of expectations about student performance, 71
  "model minorities" in the classroom, 80
  reading skills in classroom, 70
  and "role model" students, 54
  searching for the ideal kindergartner, 74–76
  teaching about diversity, 82
  use of discourse of behaviorism, 71, 83
  use of discourse of child-centeredness, 70, 79
  use of discourse of development, 75
  use of punishments in the classroom, 73–74
  use of rewards in the classroom, 72–73
  use of sociocultural discourse, 82
Nicholson. L., 104
normalization, 24
nursery schools, 22

O'Connor, J., 37, 45
Olneck, M. R., 87, 91, 92
Origin of Species (Darwin), 20
Osborn, D. K., 16, 18

Paley, V. G., 154
Paper Bag Princess, The, 143
Parent Teacher Organization (Woodlawn Elementary School), 50
  Committee on the Cultural Arts, 62
Paterson, M., 113, 140
Pestazolli, J., 17, 24
Peterson, P., 3
Peterson, P. L., 3
Phillips, D. C., 17
Piaget, J., 24

Plato, 40
Plumb, E., 31, 32, 35, 36, 44
Popkewitz, T., 54
Porter, M., 50, 51, 55, 59, 61
pre-service teachers
  prejudices among, 2
  use of reflective journals, 2
production of knowledge, 151

Quam, S., 18

Race, Identity and Representation (McCarthy and Crichlow), 104
racial oppression, 81, 87
Randall, M., 112, 114, 117, 119
  resignation of, 129
Ray, G., 39, 40, 41, 44
Reinke, L., 29, 33, 40, 41, 45
  creating supportive alliances, 41–42
Reynolds, D., 103, 104, 106
Rodriguez, N., 105, 110
"role model" students, 53, 55
Ross, E., 22
Rothman, S., 19, 23
Rousseau, J. J., 17, 24, 40

Sanchez, C., 99, 100, 104, 106, 109, 110
Schurz, M., 18
Shavelson, R., 3
Shaw, V., 122, 123, 124, 129
signs, 8
Skinner, B. F., 23
Sleeter, C. E., 87, 95, 101, 118, 120, 121, 141
Social Postmodernism, Beyond Identity Politics (Nicholson and Steidman), 104
speech genres, 7
  definition of, 9–10
  and discourses, 7
Social Darwinism, 20
  social activism, 93
  efficiency educators, 20, 21, 22
  efficiency movement, 25
  identities, 79
  studies, 2
Something Special for Me (Williams), 144
Spodek, B., 22
standardized tests, 22
Steidman, S., 104

Stern, P., 3
Stone, J., 48, 55, 57, 58
Swadener, E. B., 26

Takaki, R., 89, 90
teacher education, 2
   research on, 3
teacher identities, 150–52
teacher thinking,
   and action, 3
   as a collective enterprise, 5–6
   definition of, 39
   as a dialectic process, 3, 4–5, 6
   literature on, 3
   personal dimension of, 4
   theoretical framework for studying collective, 6–10
   social nature of, 1, 3
   study of the social nature of, 10
   as unidimensional, 3–4
teacher training programs, 19
teachers
   accountability of, 25
   awareness of the use of discourses, 154
   and biases, 37
   as "change agents," 103
   constructions of the prospective early childhood, 44–46
teaching machines, 24
Tharp, R. G., 26
Thorndike, E., 21
"tourist approach" to diversity, 62

Valdez, G., 105
Vickery, W., 90, 91
Villegas, A. M., 36
Volosinov, V., 6, 8
Vygotsky, L. S., 26

Ward, F. L., 31
Warner, S. A., 154
Watertown Historical Society, 18
Watertown, Wisconsin, 18
Watson, J. B., 23
Weber, E., 17, 20
White, A. O., 88
white flight, 113

White Teacher (Paley), 155
Wickersham, J. P., 16
Williams, G. W., 87, 88, 89
Williams, V. B., 143
Winsler, A., 26
Woodlawn Elementary School, 11, 46
   "appropriate behaviors" at, 54
   children of poverty at, 49–50
   description of students and their families, 48–49, 52–53
   high-needs children, 53
   homelessness of students, 71
   description of surrounding neighborhood, 47
   discourse of child-centeredness at, 60
   discourse of normalization at, 63
   genre of, 63–64
   kindergarten magnet program at, 51
      as a theacher directed program, 68–74
      curriculum at, 58, 59
      description of students in, 53, 66–67
      example of writing exercise, 67–68
      report card, 58–61
      student behavior in, 55
   multicultural education at, 61–62
      "tourist approach" to diversity, 62
   multiage classrooms at, 55
   Parent Cooperative, 62
   Parent Teach Organization, 50
      Committee on the Cultural Arts, 62
   parental support of,
   "planning centers" in classrooms, 61
   redistricting of, 51–52
   "role model" students at, 53, 55
   Also see Nicholi, Anne; Woodlawn Learning Center
Woodlawn Learning Center, 56
   behavioral problems at, 56
   disciplinary issues at, 57
   and discourses of domesticity, 57
   role of students' fathers, 57
Woodson, C. G., 88, 89, 90

Yolonda's Genius, 155

Zahorik, J. A., 3
Zeichner, K., 107